# A WELL SPENT JOURNEY

A BIOGRAPHY OF JAMES WOOD

TIMOTHY WOOD

INGLEWOOD

# FOREWORD

We have the tenderest memories of Jim Wood the
pastors' pastor, and are so very thankful that God's
providence was to bring us regularly into the same
orbit. What formidable graces he displayed and quite
unconsciously, Kindness, warm accessibility, patience,
good humour and godliness spring to mind, while
readily available to uphold and discuss the truth,
concerned for the self-promoter and egotist, while
deeply committed to his biblical worldview. That, he
could not compromise.

His preaching and pastoring were never self-
promoting, there was a self-effacement that
commended him and his words. He was esteemed by
all who knew him, well regarded, self-forgetful and
lowly in service. He would always give an opening word
of reflection and welcome at the annual Reformation
and Revival Conference that was simply superb, setting
the tone for the next two days of ministry, praise and

fellowship, but he was quite unaware of the impact to his words, possessing such a self-effacing view of his own gifts.

He possessed a very fine mind, discerning, knowledgeable, both of the history of the church and of those men of our day who were presenting themselves as living sacrifices to the Lord Christ. His sermons could be wry and erudite, but warm and appealing as he presented the gospel and person of Jesus to Christian and seeker alike. What a striking couple he and his wife made, handsome and modest the parents of such a loving trio of boys whose service of God came from their observation of the joy they had experienced knowing what God had done and was doing through Mum and Dad.

There was always fruit in his pastorates, and so there was grief that we could not gather at his funeral because of Covid restrictions, Many wanted to show their deep thankfulness to God for first drawing Jim Wood to Himself, and then drawing us into the circle of blessedness that we invariably enjoyed in the golden hours we spent together. He loved the Lord with all of his mind, and he used his mind to love all people. He was committed to walk in wisdom, evangelism and discipleship influencing his sons to do the same. His foundational bedrock was the gospel and his convictions and life showed all who knew him how much bigger and better the kingdom of God was than they had ever imagined. He showed me what a Christian leader should be. He brought together the timeless, immutable wisdom and gentleness of Christianity and used it to transform the broken lives he met throughout his pastoral ministry.

Geoff Thomas
September 2023

# 1

## EARLY YEARS

My father, James Wood, was born in Bolton, on the 26th of May in 1931 at the Royal Bolton Hospital, in the north of England. His parents were Samuel and Edna Wood. His father Samuel was a successful businessman and dentist and was well respected in Bolton. Edna came from a good Christian home; her mother was a wonderful Christian. While Samuel and Edna were together, Samuel led Edna to believe that he too was a Christian. However, as soon as they married, he stopped attending Church and refused to participate in Christian activities. This broke Edna's heart, but she was determined that her home would be run on Christian principles. With this in mind, she was steadfast that her two sons should accompany her to Church every Sunday, including attending Sunday School and Crusaders, a Christian youth organisation. Edna was a typical Lancashire lady: talkative, chatty, fussy, and slightly bossy. But she was not the boss at home. Sam, as she called him, was a strong-willed man, and kept his wife in line when she stepped out. Nevertheless, their marriage was a happy one despite their spiritual differences.

Peter was James' younger brother by two years. They both described their early years together as being, "not particularly close." That's not to say that they didn't get along, but they were very much chalk and cheese. James was more academic, whereas Peter was more focused on outdoor activity, playing football, and so on. However, as the years went by, their bond of brotherhood grew stronger, and they became very close. I know that James admired Peter, and Peter admired James.

James attended Devonshire Road Junior School in 1936, and then attended Bolton School. His early life was interrupted by the war. He often recalled the difficult days of rationing food and attending the Anderson Shelter in the middle of the night during air-raids, while Manchester was being bombed. Food was so scarce, that on one occasion when his father accidentally hit a rabbit while driving, he reversed to collect it, brought it home, and they ate rabbit for dinner that night. I remember saying to my grandpa, "that's a bit cruel," and him replying with, "it was the war years, and that's what you had to do."

As a result of the war, their travels were limited. However, James remembered the holidays they had, mainly in Wales on a farm. James loved sailing while on holiday, but something that came out of his holidays, that remained with James throughout his life, was his love for both horses and horse riding. On these holidays, James would spend hours horse riding with his father. James got along well with his parents, although he described his relationship with his father then, as a bit aloof. However, he was exceedingly close to his mother. From a very early age James was serious about Christian beliefs, and he and his mother would always talk about spiritual things. I remember my dad saying to me, that although his mother had a simple belief in the Bible, she made it her rule and her guide throughout her life and encouraged her sons to do the same. James always thanked God for his mother, describing her as the greatest influence on his life.

Apart from going to church every Sunday, from the age of 10, James attended Crusaders, a Christian youth organisation. He remembered his Crusader leader, Ken Mitchell, very well and how Ken taught the scriptures faithfully to the boys, week after week. He used to go to summer Crusader camps, as well as Pioneer camps, led by David Tryon, a youth worker for South Africa General Mission. The vicar at St. Peter's Church also saw his maturity and spiritual growth and encouraged him to take part in church services, especially public reading. James recalled the time that he was asked to read from 2 Kings 18:27 where the modern translation reads, "drink their own urine." James hadn't examined the passage in advance, so as he read it aloud, he reacted with a slight exclamation upon encountering a word he thought of as a swear word that caught him off guard! The vicar pulled him aside and told him, "That's why we should always read the passage before reading it publicly." This caused amusement to many members of the church; a good friend of his mother phoned her the next day and said, in a broad Lancashire accent, "I see that Jimmy learnt a new word last night!"

During the war, he heard an awful lot about his grandmother on his mother's side, Granny Moss, who was a devoted Christian. She also became a significant influence in his life. She was based in Edinburgh, working for SASRA (The Soldiers' & Airmen's Scripture Readers Association). Every Sunday evening, she would round up soldiers from the streets saying, "what are you doing tonight?" When they responded, "Nothing," she would respond, "Right, follow me. We're going to church."

Sidlow Baxter, pastor of Charlotte Baptist Chapel at the time, recalled how every Sunday evening, around 10 minutes into the service, she would enter through the church doors, followed by several soldiers. Many men came to know the Lord because of her. Although James' father at the time wasn't a Christian, he had enough people around to encourage him in his Christian walk with the Lord. I remember asking him at what age he became a Christian, and he said 5, but he went on to say that it wasn't until he was 13 that he made his total commitment to the Lord. This was because of a mission that he attended at Bolton town hall, where the speaker was Ian Thomas, who also became a great influence on James' spiritual life.

Ian Thomas was founder of Capernwray Hall, which still runs today in Lancashire, as well as many other parts of the world; here, Christians are able to register to study at the assorted Bible schools or attend a variety of camps and house-parties throughout the year. Ian Thomas was also founder of "Torchbearers international." I remember meeting him; he was introduced to me as Major Thomas. I was more intrigued about his role as a Major than as an evangelist. He served in the British Expeditionary force in Belgium, taking part in the evacuation at Dunkirk. He also served in France, Italy, and Greece. He was decorated with the Distinguished Service Order for conspicuous gallantry in taking out a German machine gun nest. When the Germans surrendered at the Battle of Monte Casino, Major Thomas took the flag of surrender. As a result of the devastation of World War II, Major Thomas returned to England with his wife, determined to open the doors for young Europeans, including Germans. This was a very bold move at the time because the Germans were resented. Yet, many young Germans came to Capernwray and called themselves, "Fackelträger," or "carriers of the torch," hence, the title of Torchbearers was born.

Both James and Ian Thomas shared a common love, that of horses and horse riding, which they spent many hours doing together. Hours were spent riding and talking about the Lord. James excelled at school, where he did well in all subjects, especially English, History, Geography and Mathematics. He didn't particularly excel in science and in sports, by his own admission. Although he didn't play many sports, he was still a keen Bolton Wanderers Football Club fan. His hero was the same as every Bolton Wanderers fan, Nat Lofthouse, who played for Bolton throughout his footballing career. Lofthouse won 33 caps for England, scoring 30 goals, with the highest goals per game ratio of any England player. In

1946, James and his brother Peter went to see Bolton play against Stoke City. Stoke City had the great Stanley Matthews playing for them, which caused both a stir and excitement at the time. Unfortunately, there was over crowding of the terraces that caused a stampede, where 33 Bolton fans were killed and 400 were injured.

At first, James saw amusing things happening. One man's bowler hat was pushed so far down his whole face that he couldn't see, and in his deep Lancashire accent he kept saying, "I can't see a bloomin' thing." But it wasn't until he saw children being passed over the heads of others that he realised something serious was happening. The game stopped for a moment, allowing the injured to be removed, but those who had died were laid along the touchline, and their bodies were subsequently covered by coats. The game was restarted, with a new sawdust lined touchline separating the players from the corpses. The bodies remained there for the entirety of the game. Stanley Matthews later said that it was one of the most sickening sights he had ever seen and was disgusted that the game was allowed to continue. James and Peter's father, Samuel, faced an agonising wait to discover if either of his sons had been killed or injured. This tragedy stayed with James for a long time. Later, as President of the Old Boltonians, James spoke about this incident at Bolton's new ground, the Reebok Stadium.

James had lots of school friends. One that remained close up to his dying days was Nigel Atherton. Nigel and James had a lot in common. Humour, intelligence, but especially their Christian stance. They weren't just school friends, they also attended the same crusader class.

Together, they helped and supported each other. Although James appeared to be well-behaved, he had his moments. I recall him telling me about the time he and a few friends were at the railway station, where some of the trains were parked for the night. They were playing around the trains and carriages. A policeman saw them, kicked the boys up the backside, and told them to go home; when he went home, he wouldn't dare mention what happened to his father.

By James' admission, although very popular with his contemporaries as a boy, he was different from them. The others liked to play football, but he loved trains, aeroplanes, and boats. His hobbies differed from the others. The other interest that perhaps made him different from others, was that of acting. James had a real love for Shakespeare, and acted in several plays such as "Hamlet" playing the part of the Gentleman, "The Devil's Disciple" as lawyer Hawkins, and other plays. I didn't know this, until my brother told me, that James could make himself cry on command. This perhaps explains how he could contain himself by keeping a straight face in bizarre situations. In times where everyone would be laughing their heads off, he wouldn't show a flicker of emotion if he didn't want to. His acting skills were so good that it was recognised by a National Dramatics Society who wanted him to be part of their team. This greatly alarmed his mother, who more often than not, interfered, worried that it would distract Jimmy's spiritual walk with the Lord.

I don't know how serious he was about acting, but even as a young boy, he took his role as a Christian seriously. So much so, that he preached his first sermon at the age of 16, at one of the local mission halls. He was recognised for his gift, and they kept asking him to preach. I remember asking him when he felt called upon to become a full-time preacher. He said that, from a very early age, he always felt that he should go into full-time Christian work. He shared this with his vicar, who again was supportive of him.

At first, he felt it was missionary work. St Peter's had a flow of missionaries, and he loved hearing their reports when they came back to England. He was very keen to go to India. I only learned this later when I went to visit India myself. This drive to be a missionary explains why he later became so missionary-minded. I remember him telling me about the time he told his parents of his goal to enter full-time Christian work. It was just after dinner with his mother and father. His father had big ambitions for his son, having seen a lot of potential in him. He had hoped he would become a solicitor. I'm not sure how old James was, but when he told them, a disgusted father put his napkin on the table, and walked out, leaving behind a very uncomfortable atmosphere, and a shocked son. Clearly disapproving of his son's intentions in life, his father shook his head with disbelief as he left. Helplessly, James looked at his mother who immediately said, "remember what it says in the Bible: 'he who honours me, I will honour him.'" Unknown to them both at the time, James' calling became the turning point in his father's spiritual life. Still disturbed by his father's disapproval, he turned to Major Thomas for advice in the Christian ministry. Major Thomas encouraged him to leave this matter with the Lord. In the meantime, James attended Christian Camps, beach missions, and was involved in many Christian activities, such as working at Capernwray Hall. Before he could enter full-time Christian service, James had another hurdle to face: National Service.

In 1949 James received his National Service call-up papers. To whom should he turn for advice, as a young Christian, on how to serve the Lord while in the Army? Well, who was better equipped than Major Ian Thomas?

## 2

## ARMY LIFE

IT WAS ESSENTIAL FOR JAMES TO MAINTAIN NOT ONLY HIS spiritual walk with the Lord, but to be a living testimony to other soldiers, as a witness to them. In many ways, this would be a good training ground for James. Having had a somewhat sheltered life, coming from a good stable home, he now had to learn about the "big, bad world." When he entered the army, this was a critical period world-wide. The Second World War may have finished but there were new tensions. The Iron Curtain had been declared by Winston Churchill in 1946. It was a non-physical boundary dividing Europe into two separate areas after the Second World War, until the end of the Cold War in 1991. Then followed the 1950 Korean War. Germany was divided into four parts: the American zone, the French zone, the British sector of the West, and the Russians in the East. When James was eventually based in Germany, he told me that he could often see the Russians, through their telescopes, and saw them as a menacing threat. He also believed that, had they moved towards the West, the West would have had no chance in stopping them.

Just before James left for the Army, an unexpected turn of events happened which brought great joy to the family. James' father had struggled for some time with his son's calling and started to attend meetings at St Peter's Church. They had a mission where, again, Major Ian Thomas was the speaker. One evening, Samuel Wood entered the room where James and his mother were sitting, and put his cigarettes and lighter on the table and announced, "I won't be needing this anymore." This, of course, made them turn around, but it was what he said next that shocked them.

"I have become a Christian."

Samuel Wood had committed his life to the Lord. In gratitude to God and thankful for Major Thomas, he offered to become Major Thomas' driver for evangelistic meetings. He later became a Gideon and was responsible for the distribution of Gideon's Bibles in the North West.

James joined the 8th Royal Tank Regiment in August 1950. The Royal Tank Regiment's motto was, "Fear Naught." Originally, the regiment came about during the First World War in 1916. It changed its name to the Royal Tank Corps in 1939. By now, the British Army was a respected force in the world and so was the Royal Tank Regiment. They had produced tanks of their own that were well recognised. James' first training was in Tilshead, Wiltshire, based in the centre of the Salisbury Plain. He was given his uniform and was instructed on the importance of discipline. Uniforms had to be pressed neatly, boots polished, and short hair was mandatory.

Like everyone else, he endured hours of marching and then basic training. He so impressed his superiors, that while in Tilshead he received his first stripe to become Lance Corporal Wood. The next stage of training was learning to drive lorries and scout cars. He was sent to Bovington Camp in Dorset for tank training. This was where he learnt to drive the Centurion Tank.

He also trained as a wireless communicator. As part of his training, he drove the German Tiger 131 as well as the British Mk I used during the First World War. James was in his element. He always wanted to fly planes, but driving a tank was the next best thing. I remember asking him what it was like to drive a tank. He simply said, "hard work." To steer the tank, you had to use levers. You didn't use a steering wheel. The levers required particular strength and the machinery of the tank was heavy. It also had a five-man crew and teamwork and bonding were crucial. But even while he was in the Army, James was living a Christian life and maintaining his walk with the Lord. I asked him if he had a hard time in the Army as a Christian. He explained that he was teased, but overall, he was respected.

For instance, he always held onto the belief that just before his dinner, he should say grace. One day he said grace and opened his eyes to find that his dinner plate had disappeared. All the other soldiers were amused by this, and one tapped him on the shoulder and said, "remember what the old book says, 'watch and pray.'" He told me that he never did get his dinner back that night!

It was while he was in Tilshead that he met a young man named Ted Ellis. Ellis was a lonely figure and with

James feeling sorry for him , he spoke to him. Ted Ellis asked why he was showing concern for him. James replied that he was a Christian and that's what Christians do, they look out for others. James had the privilege of leading Ted to the Lord. Ted always stayed in contact with James, even coming to visit our family once a year. His visits decreased when we moved to London, but he still kept in touch.

After 3 months of training in England, James was sent to Germany. He was sent to Paderborn, a city in western Germany. It was a long journey, where he took a train to Harwich, and from Harwich to Hoek van Holland (Or Hook/Corner of Holland), a small town in Southern Netherlands, located directly across from Harwich. From there, he took a train to Paderborn station. James was in his element, travelling on one of his favourite interests, steam trains. Those who knew James, know how passionate he was about steam trains. My brothers and I tried to show an interest in them ourselves, but we couldn't quite get into it. Later in life, as a hobby, he used to make model steam trains and carriages, some of which were on display in his house, until he passed away. According to him, the Germans were ahead of their time when it came to the making of steam trains; that's why he enjoyed the journey to Paderborn so much. When the train pulled in, James put his kit bag over his shoulders and along with the other soldiers, stepped out of the carriage into the sound of steam, whistles from the train, and the noise of soldiers and people.

In 1950, Germany was a subdued nation and seeing people in uniform would cause them to turn and move away, with weary and defeatist looks. The noisy soldiers were guided out of the station where army trucks were waiting to take them to their camp, Barker Barracks. When I asked, I remember him explaining to me why it wasn't a very German-sounding name. It was originally called "Westfalen Garrison," and had been home to the German Panzer division back in the 1930s. It was renamed by the British, after General Sir Evelyn Barker. These barracks were under British rule and were home for the 20th Armoured Brigade, the 5th Dragoon Guards, and the 8th Royal Tank Regiment.

The barracks were huge, with a large ground area for both marching and tank parades. Regular, daily exercise was routine, and James made it very clear that he did not like the PT instructors. He explained that they were over the top with their constant shouting, name-calling and crude language. He told me that they were despised more than the military police and, jokingly, the Scots Guards. When I asked him about the Scots Guards, he said, "if there was an exercise that involved them, and you were caught, they would beat you up."

Discipline was heavy while in Germany. Daily barrack inspections, including uniform checks, were the routine. Trousers had to be pressed neatly, with uniforms laid out at the end of a well-made bed, with the Sergeant Major coming down hotly at any sign of a crease. This probably explains why James was such a well-dressed person in later life. Daily parades and hours of marching were also routine. Then there were the lectures he attended. These lectures covered hygiene and discipline, as well as lessons on tank driving. One set of lectures

James had to listen to, were those about the war, with veterans telling them of their experiences in tank battles. These he found fascinating. He also had to listen to lectures about the Germans and their people, and how they should be approached and what to expect from them. As far as the British and the Allies were concerned, although the war had been finished for five years at this point, the Germans were still the enemies, and they were to be treated with suspicion.

He also attended a lecture on German women, warning of prostitution. Of course, this was a shock to James. Having led a very sheltered life, he wasn't used to this kind of talk. Unfortunately, he saw this was a way of life for some of the soldiers. He had another lecture on the evil of Nazism. This, I believe, had a significant effect on him. It was not helped by the visit to Belsen, a former German concentration camp. Belsen was a 2-hour journey from Paderborn and most British troops had to visit there, not just to hear about the evil of Nazism, but to see it for themselves. Although the camp of Belsen had been largely destroyed by the British, there were parts of it at the time that remained, for example, the cremators. James hated the Nazis and had no time for those who later tried to twist history by saying that the Allies went too far. I once asked him about the bombing of Dresden towards the end of the war, "What about Dresden, don't you think we went too far?" Quickly he turned to me and replied, "What about Coventry? What about London? What about Liverpool and Stalingrad? What about the Jews?" I got the point pretty quickly.

Once they had been told all that they needed to know

and what to expect, the soldiers had to go out on patrols. At first, they had to go out in scout cars. Being the reliable and dependable person that he was, he was often asked to lead a patrol group or scout car. He was seen as so reliable that he received his second stripe as a full Corporal. Finally, it was time to go out in their tanks.

Tanks had to go out on "exercises," so the Germans could see, and the Russians knew, they weren't just sitting idly in their camps. They had to be seen to be active. Sometimes, this meant going away for the day, other times it meant multiple days, sometimes weeks. The main exercise was preparing for tank battle. This might sound fun for the adventurous young boy, but it was hard work. The mud on the Rhine fields, in extremely cold conditions, was a hard task. However, James enjoyed his days driving tanks, away from his superior officers, and amongst friends. For James, there was no greater feeling than standing by your tank, with your crew, waiting for an order, and then jumping into your tank, putting on your headphones, the sound of tanks roaring and the smell of diesel filling the air, following all the other tanks out of camp. He held the privilege once of taking his tank over Arnhem Bridge, which was known as the place where, during the Second World war, Operation Market Garden had taken place. This was of particular interest for James because his father's cousin was General Horrocks, one of the commanders of Monty's team, who planned Operation Market Garden.

One instance, his tank crew had spent all night in a field. When they woke up the next morning, they could see that they were near a farm. The commander instructed James to drive up to the farm. The farmer came out of the farmhouse, and the commander of the tank said to the farmer, "Bacon and eggs for the men and me." The farmer protested and said, "No, no food." The commander then ordered James, "Corporal, turn on your engine, and drive straight through that barn." The farmer protested, waving his hands shouting, "okay, okay!" Eventually food was provided to them. Once again, I mentioned how it sounded quite harsh, but he responded to me and said, "They would have done exactly the same to us."

James not only saw the evil of Nazism, but he also saw the devastation of war. Buildings destroyed, towns flattened, cities and villages bore all the hallmarks of war. He saw more of this when he was stationed a few times in Berlin. Berlin, like Germany, was also divided into four zones: British, American, French, and Russian. Since Berlin was in the East, the Allies insisted that Berlin also be split, with the French taking the North, the British in the centre, and the Americans in the South. Going to Berlin, meant going through the Russian Sector, which the Russians guarded enviously. The glares of distrust from all parties were menacing; so much so, the crew would say to James, "Say a prayer for us." Although this was just a joke to them, it showed that he had a testimony before the soldiers. Berlin was very tense, especially a year after the Berlin airlift, which lasted 323 days (26th June 1948 – 30th September 1949). Stalin was still alive and there were food shortages and soldiers everywhere. It was known as the Capital of Spies, but it was the ruins of Berlin that caught James' attention the most. I remember going to Berlin in 1969 when we stayed with SASRA workers, a godly couple named Jim and Martha Waring. It was tense even then. If it was tense then, I can only imagine how hostile it would have felt for James at the time.

James said that when he went to Berlin 20 years later, there was a slight improvement, only this time, the Berlin Wall had been built. One should remember that, had there been a war, James would have undoubtedly been on the frontline; tanks don't just slip into the background, they are put right in the centre of the battleground.

I remember once asking him if he ever suspected that there might be another war, maybe with the Russians. He told me, "Well, there was one occasion that I thought it was a real possibility. It was one late afternoon, and we were in the engine room at Barker Barracks, when suddenly a siren sound deafened the entire base. Everyone started running across the parade ground, engines were being started, men were running to their vehicles, when the Sergeant came in and shouted, 'this is no practice drill, get in your vehicles, start your engines, and wait for further instructions!' We all ran to our tanks, started the engines, and drove towards the entrance followed by other vehicles, and then we waited. As I looked at the chaos and shouting going on, mixed with the loud siren, I thought, could this really be it? To this day, I do not know whether it was real or just practice."

After a while, James was able to prove his worth. While he learnt to ski and ice-skate, he was most pleased to do what he loved: ride regimental horses. His talents as a rider were recognized as he was asked if he wanted to join the Household Cavalry. However, he declined.

But, James was a Christian. He didn't allow the Army life to distract his walk with the Lord. He explained that life in the army, as a Christian, was tough. It wasn't so much the bantering or ridicule from his fellow soldiers that he found difficult; in fact, his fellow soldiers admired him for his faith but it was finding the time and the place for quietness with which he battled. I asked him how he managed, and he said that he always carried a pocket Bible with him, along with a note pad. Every day, he had his daily devotions and said his prayers. His Christian position was so clear, he was asked to be the official Lay Reader to the Padre.

When his time was up in the army, his talents were recognised in that his superiors advised him to go on an officer's course to try and make a career out of the Army, with prospects of promotion. He declined because he had his heart set on Christian ministry. However, he believed that the army life was good training for him, and the ministry. While he wouldn't necessarily suggest that you must join the army before going into the ministry, or any full time Christian work, he did believe that every Christian trainee ought to have some understanding of life and people. He didn't agree with men going into the ministry straight from university, or straight from school into Bible College. He believed that an understanding of the secular world should be part of their training. For James, the Army was his training ground.

# 3

## BIBLE COLLEGE

WHEN JAMES HAD SOME TIME OFF, HE RETURNED TO England in search of which Bible college he should attend. Coming from a Church of England background, he was tempted to go to Tyndale Hall in Bristol. One of the reasons that attracted him to this college was the well-known theologian, Jim Packer. He went to visit Tyndale Hall, with an purposeful outlook. But James' belief on infant baptism had changed. In fact, his whole view on the Church of England had changed.

Whilst based in Salisbury, he decided – I believe on the advice of someone who was concerned for him – to go to Duke Street Baptist Church. Duke Street was a well-known Baptist Church in Richmond, Surrey. On his first Sunday there, he entered the building not knowing a single soul. He was immediately greeted by a delightful couple, a brother and sister. Mr and Miss Turnbull said, "You must come back for lunch". He did and was virtually adopted by this delightful couple on his many Sundays at Duke Street. James' background had been in the Church of England, but here, under the ministry of Alan Redpath, James came to a conviction regarding believers' baptism by immersion. It was at Duke Street that he was baptised. James' mother supported him fully in this change of perspective. The only reason why she went to a Church of England was because for her, it was the only church that preached the Bible. She was not held down by tradition or family roots, her view was progress in the Christian life.

During a holiday in Bournemouth, James attended Lansdowne Road where a baptismal service was taking place. Francis Dixon was the Pastor there, and James worked with him for a month. Dixon recognised James' talents, and asked James to be his assistant, especially since James shared with him, his sense of calling. But James declined because he had been to visit London Bible College (LBC) and felt compelled to go there.

By this time, he was in correspondence with a certain lady, Ailsa Howarth. He had always known Ailsa from his childhood days. Ailsa's mother died when Ailsa was only a young girl; both she and James' mum had been good friends. Ailsa also attended Bolton School, but that was all. Both James and Ailsa were greatly helped in their Christian growth by attending Crusader youth groups. Now known as Urban Saints, these were established in north London in 1900 with the aim of helping young people with no real church attachment to grow in their knowledge of the Bible.

Yet their meeting up again happened not in Bolton, but in Edinburgh. Ailsa went to The Edinburgh College of Domestic Science (simply known as Atholl Crescent due to its location), in 1951. She was also a keen Christian. Although her parents were Church of England goers, and attended twice every Sunday, they were perhaps a little bit of a hindrance to her growth. They felt that Ailsa had taken her Christian faith too far. She went to college in Edinburgh to study domestic science, but this really wasn't where she wanted to go. Her love was for sports, and she wanted to become a sports teacher, but her father wasn't in favour of this. In many ways, going to Edinburgh was an escape for her, not that she disliked home, she just wanted the chance to flourish and grow in her spiritual life. Whilst in Edinburgh, she went to Charlotte Chapel, where she was baptised by the Pastor, Sidlow Baxter, much to the disapproval of her father, who did not give his blessing. Sidlow became a good family friend and, many years later when my brother Jonathan visited his home in Santa Barbara, California, he asked how "the queen of manse" (my mum) was doing! She loved her time at Charlotte Chapel, getting involved in the activities and mingling with people she described as "wonderful Christians."

Now James, while on National Service, had to go to Edinburgh. Of course, having Sunday free, he wanted to go to Charlotte Chapel to hear Sidlow Baxter. For him, it was the natural place to go since his grandmother had been based there while working for SASRA. It was here that he was re-acquainted with Ailsa. They renewed their friendship by correspondence. However, at first, Ailsa did not want James to be her boyfriend, not because he wasn't good looking or nice, but because she considered him to be too holy, and believed he would spoil her fun!

However, Ailsa always felt that she too had some Christian calling, and they shared this together. James shared with her his longing to go to the London Bible College (LBC) and into the Christian Ministry. Ailsa believed he was doing the right thing, and the relationship then blossomed.

Then James, one day, went on a walk with Ailsa, up Arthur's Seat, the hill right in the heart of Edinburgh that overlooks the city. It was the same hill that Robert Louis Stevenson describes as, "a hill for magnitude, a mountain in virtue of its bold design," and there, he proposed to her. But, before they should marry, they agreed that James should complete his studies at LBC.

Going to LBC gave James some of the best days of his life. London did not faze James, especially for a northerner. In fact, he loved London. For James, London was a place of opportunity, a place of fine buildings, art, and culture. Of course, that was not his purpose in going to London. Going to London was to prepare for Christian Ministry. He entered Bible College with a great deal of enthusiasm, and he was not disappointed. London Bible College wasn't that old in existence at the time. It opened in 1944, but the first full time students started their studies in 1946. The first Principal was Ernest Kevan. Ernest Kevan was an incredible theologian. He was recommended to the staff of LBC to be appointed as Principal by Dr Martyn Lloyd-Jones. Coming under such a recommendation, the faculty could not refuse to appoint him, and they were not disappointed. Ernest Kevan was loved by all the students. In fact, James said that after his mother and his wife, Ernest Kevan was the greatest influence on his life.

Ernest Kevan came from a strict Baptist background, pastoring churches mainly in the London area. Other members of the staff included the great theologian Donald Guthrie and Dermot MacDonald. It was through Ernest Kevan that James had thoughts about the works of the Puritans. He had heard about the Puritans and the works they did, but he hadn't really studied them enough. Ernest Kevan encouraged all his students to study them. James' love for the Puritans stemmed from there. Another benefit for James while in London was his visits to Westminster Chapel, to hear the great Welsh preacher Dr Martyn Lloyd Jones. The 1950s were a difficult decade for evangelicalism in Britain. It had survived the difficult war period, lives had been shattered, there was a collapse of morality, people overall were disappointed with the social concern, and there was a rise of liberalism.

Liberalism had been on the rise since the days of Spurgeon's downgrade controversy, just as Spurgeon predicted. The Church of England, Methodists, and the Baptist Union had all allowed liberals to have their say. On top of that, there was a shallow approach towards Christianity. It was all focused on campaigns, crusades, and missions. Not that this was wrong, just that the need for living holy lives and the depths of Christian teaching were not emphasised enough. Yet, it was through the steady influence of Lloyd-Jones, that things would begin to change. He believed this would be accomplished through good preaching.

By "good preaching," he meant expository preaching, where the scriptures would be expanded upon and explained, letting scripture speak for itself. This was something that James grasped very quickly and latched onto. By now, every Friday, Dr. Lloyd Jones was preaching at Westminster Chapel. It was regularly packed with 2,500 people. I remember some years later; I went with James to hear a lecture at the Evangelical Library held in the back hall of Westminster Chapel. I had asked if we could go and look around the Chapel. He took me up into the gallery and reminisced on how full it used to be, so much so that people would sit on the window ledges. It was one of the few times I saw him choke up, where he couldn't continue to speak because he was so overwhelmed by the memory of it. He told me of one occasion, where he had to listen to a lecture while at college, and found the subject long and dreary. So, when he went to the chapel that night and Dr. Lloyd Jones announced the very same text, he thought that he wouldn't get anything out of it. However, he was very wrong and left the service praising God.

Ernest Kevan insisted that his students were not just there to learn theology and listen to lectures, but they were there to "do." He got them involved in local churches, including children's work and missions, and every Sunday they were to preach around London. James did so, and he loved it. I remember some 30 years later, when I went to Bible College and had to do the same at London Theological Seminary. I would preach at different churches in London, and people would come up to me after the service and say, "Are you James Wood's son? He used to stay with us."

Along with theological studies of scriptures, lectures included the importance of hygiene, manners, Greek. But among all these things, there was another love that James had while at Bible College: fellowship and friendship. He spoke fondly of his Bible College friends, Keith Mawdsley, Phil Holder, Eddie Prest, and others. His friendships were lasting, especially with Keith to whom he remained close until the day he died.

After four years of studying, his time at LBC came to an end. He was sad at this departure, but was eager for the next chapter of his life: marriage and his first church.

In 1956, Ailsa and Jim married at Ailsa's home Parish Church in Bolton. In the same year, James was called to the railway town of Crewe, to West Street Baptist Church. The church owned a house that had the grand title of The Manse, but it wasn't very grand. In fact, Ailsa wept when she first saw her new, and first home, that she described as, "dilapidated, neglected, gardenless, with an old kitchen from the iron age, wobbly tiles on the floor, a coal bunker in the yard, and in a cheerless, sunless location."

Her father resented the fact that she married a Baptist minister, and far from being impressed, quipped "what do you expect from a Baptist?"

**4**

---

# CREWE

THE TOWN OF CREWE IS PRIMARILY KNOWN AS A RAILWAY town. In fact, historically it was one of the most significant railway stations in the world. The station was opened in 1837, and it was intended to be the rail gateway for the North and West. It ran upwards to Manchester and Glasgow and would diverge to North Wales. Crewe was chosen as the major junction because it was the central link for the four largest cities of England, joining the existing Liverpool and Manchester railway with the projected London and Birmingham railway. It was such a busy station that in 1900, it was recorded that in 24 hours, 1,000 trains would pass through on a daily basis. Half of these were freight trains. So, we are not just talking about a very large station, but we are also talking about the area which included signal boxes and junctions. It wasn't just a place where people stopped to change to either Manchester, Liverpool, Glasgow or to London, but it was also the place where mail parcels and other supplies would be stationed to their destinations.

Today, it has twelve platforms. But Crewe isn't only known for being a large railway junction; at one time it was also the home of Rolls Royce motor car production. So, the majority of workers were men who worked at the railway, for Rolls Royce, or for the Post Office. For this reason, it was a bit of a downtrodden town, of working-class people. The other important factor about Crewe, was that it was surrounded by beautiful Cheshire countryside, where farmers had the luxury of good green land, perfect for dairy farming (that's why Crewe also provided a very big agricultural college) along with Nantwich.

When James arrived in Crewe, it had a population of about 50,000. It wasn't a big town, but neither was it too small. It was a community where most people knew what was going on. This played a significant part in James' role when he came to Crewe. Primarily, he went to Crewe to be Pastor of West Street Baptist Church, to preach the gospel. However, his reputation grew in the community and he was viewed as a man of stature in the community. That's why he was asked to join several committees in Crewe, like school councils, probation service, hospital work, and even later as a magistrate.

A second crucial point that helps to set the scene is to note that Crewe was very much a run-down area. There were lots of streets with terraced houses, and areas looking more like bomb sites. People prided themselves on being working class. West Street Baptist Church was located right in the middle of these terraced houses. For a newly wedded couple, from the middle-class area of Bolton, this was a challenge. Yet, this newly wedded couple were so committed to the cause of the gospel, that they devoted themselves entirely to the work. I'm not sure how James first came into contact with Crewe. It may have been that the church asked LBC if they would recommend him or it may have been thanks to a recommendation from someone else. However, the West Street Baptist Church's secretary, a certain Jack Maybury, recalled the very time when he first saw this man.

A Sunday had been arranged for James to come and preach, and Jack went to meet him at Crewe station. You can imagine the scene as Jack waited for him. The station noise, people getting on and off the train, all while Jack searched for this man. Finally, Jack saw this very smartly dressed young man, wearing a bowler hat and a camel coat, a dog collar visible underneath, smartly pressed trousers, shining shoes, and a neatly folded umbrella under his arm. Jack said that he looked more like a city worker, far away from the working-class Crewe. Jack thought to himself, "is this man serious?"

This was not about first impressions for James, it was simply his way of life. Having a smart dress code was what he lived by for his entire life. In fact, I have heard it said that he was the smartest man in Christendom in pressed trousers, polished shoes, and always wearing a tie. Even during family holidays or gardening, he would wear a tie.

At first, Jack Maybury's concern was whether this was the right man for the area? Yet, the two men got along like a house on fire. When he finally preached, they were so impressed with his talents and enthusiasm that they called him to be their Pastor in 1956, when he was ordained and inducted. At the induction service Ernest

Kevan preached, and the Charge to the Minister was made by L.S. Watson, the area superintendent.

The church provided for them a manse on Samuel Street, just around the corner of West Street. It was not an ideal house for anyone, let alone a newly wedded couple. Every room in the house was damp with wallpaper hanging off the walls. If the house was run down, the state of the church building was no better. Nevertheless, this young couple got to work making the best use of what they had, painting, scrubbing the floors and walls, tidying, and cleaning up as much as possible. For Ailsa this was hard. While it was hard for James, at least he had the training of the army. Moreover, Crewe was the ideal place for this train enthusiast, car-loving man; he could relate to people so well. However, their first task wasn't relating to the people - it was the gospel. Yet, to open the doors for the gospel, they had to be seen as workers in the community. That's why James had a very strong belief in visitation. For me, his visitation programme was very regimental. Every morning was taken up with sermon preparation, and every afternoon he would go out visiting.

What also made the work hard for James and Ailsa was the spiritual state of the church, or the lack thereof. It was a Baptist Union Church with a membership of 16; Sunday morning attendance on average was about 12. According to my brother Jonathan, an average Sunday evening service consisted of about 7. The building was large, with a big old pipe organ and gallery at the back with a huge pulpit. Imagine the sight of James preaching amongst such a small group of people! Another problem was the lack of spiritual life. James said that he believed only three of them were truly saved. This was further proved by the opposition he faced, when James' uncompromising stance on preaching the gospel was opposed, with no help from the Baptist Union.

One man, Mr. Farrell, who had a garage business, violently opposed everything James tried to do. Things came to a head when James had to discipline this man, because he was touching women inappropriately. It came to a disciplinary matter, which made it extremely unpleasant for this new couple. Another issue this young couple had to face was poverty. The church didn't have much income to pay their Pastor and the young couple couldn't make ends meet.

Without the help of their parents and good friends, they clearly couldn't have survived. As such, they took on practical ways to help with finances. They rented a room in their home to a lodger, which helped pay the way, with the lodger living in the front room downstairs. Bear in mind this was a two-bedroom house. In 1958, their first son, Jonathan, was born. 18 months later they had their second son, Marcus, in 1959. They now had 2 children, little money, opposition in the church and little help. Yet, James and Ailsa were hard workers, and with their love for the gospel, they were determined to persevere. Knowing that they would be opposed by the older generation, they turned to children's work, and young people's work.

Slowly and gradually, the work they were doing with children and young people began to grow. Then came a turning point. A man named Keith Hockenull was converted under James' ministry. This encouraged some of the keener people at church, and things started to look up.

In 1962, their third son, Timothy (the author), was born. From the very moment Timothy was born, he gave his parents difficulties. In fact, just a few days after Timothy was born, James was preparing to preach, when a policeman came to church and strongly advised him not to preach but instead, go to the hospital as soon as possible, as the baby was now fighting for his life.

James naturally was concerned, but felt duty bound first to preach the gospel. He then rushed straight to the hospital as soon as he had finished. Due to the complications surrounding the days after his birth, Timothy was left severely hearing impaired throughout his life. The early years of Timothy's life were difficult for James because it wasn't until he was 5 years old that Timothy was diagnosed as hearing impaired. This meant constant visits to the hospital and hearing clinics, and battles with local educational authorities.

During that time, opposition remained persistent at the church. While the work was beginning to turn, and people were starting to visit the church, James was opposed by the older generation. On one occasion James went into the pulpit and opened the Bible, and out fell a note of obscene nature, calling him all sorts of names. The resignation of a prominent church member at a lively church meeting was promptly accepted by the pastor. Another church member suggested that this was done all too quickly and that James shouldn't accept his resignation in a hasty way. James' response was that, "he has obviously thought about it and prayed about it, so he has done the right thing." No one could answer back to that.

Due to his strict regimental visitation programme, persistent preaching of the word, and hard work, some of the remaining older members were won over, and became loyal, hard workers. The Sunday School grew, young people were coming and being saved, and this began to change the church, so much so that it was the young people that turned on those that opposed James' ministry, in support of his work. In fact, an amusing story came from this. The younger people christened a toy monkey naming him after a particularly awkward church member. They would place "Gilbert" in different positions around the church so that, when James was preaching to the congregation, he would see the monkey placed in the gallery one week, and then the next week, the monkey placed next to the organ, the communion table, and so on!

James began to have missions for the Children's work, where the Children's Christian Crusade (CCC) would come. This reputation grew, and people who lived in the countryside or the outskirts of Crewe would travel into town to attend. One man, who worked for Rolls Royce, was recommended by Dr Lloyd Jones to come to the church in Crewe. The gentleman, Reg Shore, used to be a member at Westminster Chapel. After attending he proved to be a valuable worker, not only a doer, but someone who could help in preaching as well.

With conversions, came baptisms, and that meant that the baptistry was opened for perhaps the first time in years. Two amusing stories came about as a result. One was with regard to the baptistry pool. Since it was old, the individual responsible for the baptistry had to be in the church to make sure that the water reached the right level. However, it was very slow to fill, so slow that he fell asleep. When he woke, water was overflowing. Naturally, he pulled the plug out using the long chain. But with the water flowing down the drain so fast, the plug wouldn't go into the hole, no matter how many times he tried. So, he had no choice but to strip down, get into the pool and put the plug back in. When he got out, he discovered there was no towel, and so the only way to dry himself was to run around the church building in just his pants!

The second story involves James' baptistry gown. Since it hadn't been used in a while, moths had got to it and created little holes. When James entered the water, he could feel the water flowing in through the gown. When he got out again, the water came out too. It must have been a very funny sight to those watching, as it was said he looked like he was relieving himself!

Due to the growth in the church, James' reputation in Crewe expanded. He was a strong supporter of the railway mission on the other side of the town. The workers of the mission loved it when he went to preach to them and support their work. It was as a result of the Railway Mission that he met Jack Mills. Jack Mills was a train driver from Crewe, who regularly stopped his train on the West Coast main line. It was here where the Great Train Robbery occurred. Though the gang did not use firearms, Jack Mills was beaten over the head with a metal bar. His injuries were so severe that not only did it end his career, but he was never the same again. Although Jack died 7 years later, James felt that the gang had murdered Jack, as he died at the young age of 58.

James was asked to join several committees in the local area, and was even asked to be a magistrate. He declined a lot of them, because he felt it would be too distracting, with his number one priority being to preach to his flock. Nevertheless, he was seen largely as a community man, the gentleman who lived in the heart of Crewe. This changed slightly when they moved away from Samuel Street to Wistaston on the outskirts of the town. James and Ailsa never complained to anyone about the state of the so-called, "grand manse," although they may have done so to each other. I know years later they laughed about some of the things they had to face, but by and large, they were kept poor, and had few luxuries.

The lack of money meant a tight budget and a need to accept help from wherever it came. There was a man in the church by the name of Fred Skurusky, who had been in a prisoner of war camp during the second world war, where his job was to cut the hair of the other prisoners. He offered his services to cut the boys' hair, and used the same brutal methods on the three of them that he had used in those prison days during the war! We would come away from his house, seeing a smile of satisfaction at the job he had done on his face as the tears rolled down our faces at the sheer pain of it all! On one occasion we all complained and were suitably chastised for our bad behaviour and ingratitude for such a kind man's actions!

The time came when James' father had had enough

of seeing the family's struggles, and as far as he was concerned the Manse was not good enough for a young family with three children. Unknown to James, and certainly without his permission, his father went to the church secretary and said, "look, you are going to lose him." The next day, the church secretary found him with several papers on houses for sale. Even when the new house was in view, the church hesitated over its purchase. A Manchester-based Christian businessman, who was also a good family friend, said that if the church did not buy it, then he would. The prevarication ended! It wasn't long before James moved away from Samuel Street, to improved conditions.

James' ministry wasn't just focused on Crewe. He met with other ministers from the Cheshire area, including Rev. John Waterman from Wheelock Heath, and Rev. Clive Tyler from Alsager Congregational Church. Then he met with others from the Northwest like, Rev. Stuart Olyott and Rev. Percy Nutall from Liverpool. They used to attend conferences together and LBC reunions. Sharing time with pastors also meant sharing suffering. One example was when John Waterman's 5 year old son tragically died of meningitis. If it wasn't hard enough for James to share their pain with this godly couple, John and Mary, he was then asked to conduct the funeral. A specific memory that stayed with James, was when he looked out at the congregation as they sang a hymn, and he saw Mary and John in the front row singing their hearts out to "There's a friend for little children above the bright blue sky"!!

James' ministry began to spread, and in 1969 he was

asked to go to America, to preach in Santa Barbara, California. He and Ailsa loved their time out there and loved the church where he was based. The church had a very large congregation of around 5,000 people. After preaching there, he was surprised to receive a call to be the associate Pastor alongside Pastor Keith Hood, an old friend from his days in Bolton. James had received many callings from different places and did not feel any of them to be right for him. As a young boy he was even asked to work alongside the evangelist Tom Rees and Francis Dixon from Lansdowne Road. However, he was seriously considering accepting the offer from the church in Santa Barbara. After prayerful thought, he declined because he was deeply focused on the ministry in Crewe. Sometime after, he heard that the pastor's wife left her husband for the choir master of the church, thus causing a split in the church. James said he was thankful that he didn't accept the call to America.

On another occasion a delegation had been sent from a Baptist Church in Winnipeg, Canada. They had heard about James' ministry and believed it was the kind they would like in their church. At the time, this was an attractive proposition, and one that James considered very seriously. The problem was that he was required to adhere to their view on the second coming of Christ, which was different from the view he held himself. He protested that he would never make an issue of the Lord's return but this proved to be insufficient for the church in Winnipeg and an end was put to that discussion. This was disheartening to James as things at Crewe were somewhat discouraging at that particular time.

Meanwhile in Crewe, the church continued to grow. From my point of view, I don't ever recall the early days at West Street as I was just a small boy. As far as I remember, the children's work, young people's work, and the size of the congregations were large. Between 1965 until the end of James' ministry at Crewe, an average evening service held over 200 people. A real sense of spiritual awakening had taken place, and James was honoured by the Lord to have witnessed conversions and blessings. Those who had opposed him from the early days had either left or had been won over and shared in the joy of seeing the remarkable things that had happened there.

However, it wasn't all plain sailing. In 1966, in a meeting of the Evangelical Alliance, Dr Lloyd Jones had announced a call out from denominations of those who compromised with the truth. The church was still in the Baptist Union, and James wasn't much of a Baptist Union man. In 1971, Dr Michael Taylor, who at the time was principal of the Northern Baptist College in Manchester, effectively denied the deity of Jesus Christ in an address to the annual assembly of the Baptist Union. This set alarm bells ringing for James, as it did for many evangelicals within the Baptist Union.

After much soul searching, James left the B.U. and took West Street Baptist out of it too. This caused upset for many supporters of the B.U., especially due to their support for a B.U. missionary, Valerie Hamilton, a missionary in East Pakistan, which is now commonly known as Bangladesh. Despite this, Valerie was so focused on her work that she didn't give the B.U. much thought, which is why the church continued to support her. The church supported many missionaries including a Bible College friend Bill Barkley who went to Brazil, Phil Holder, Roland Knight for MAF, and Jim and Martha Waring for SASRA. These are important to mention now, because they had a later impact in James' ministry.

Growth also meant dealing with unsavoury characters. I feel I must mention this because it always stayed with me, right from the beginning. My brother Jonathan reminded me, that it wasn't only due to Dad's ministry that the church grew, but that it was due to the young people's leaders. He said that many of these leaders were "doers." Some of these leaders were converted under James' ministry, while others came to Crewe, liked the ministry, and knew that James would give them his strong support. In many ways, I am reluctant to mention names, except for one couple called Simon and Sue Young.

According to Jonathan, Simon was anything but working class, but he was brilliant with people, especially young people. He was willing to witness to unsavoury and challenging people, and through him one particular family started to come to West Street. As can be expected, some conversions meant there was baggage that came with specific individuals. One of the brothers, named Jim, had done prison time, but he was saved. He had a brother called Sean. I remember Sean as a big strong man, who often carried me on his shoulders, and would play fight with me. When I heard he was going to live with us for a short time, I was thrilled. He was homeless and had nowhere to go, so James and Ailsa put him up. The trouble was, he began to steal things from around the house and started selling them. One day, James had a call from one of the jewellers and he said he had a man with him who was trying to sell one of James' watches, and asked James to check that he still had his watch on him. James realised that it had gone, and he was now in a dilemma. He felt that the police should be informed, and as such, they came to arrest Sean at our house. There was a massive argument, and scuffle, and Sean said that he wanted to kill James. Sean managed to pick up a brick with which he intended to hit James. The police had him handcuffed and he made all sorts of threats to James, saying that he was going to kill his youngest son. James obviously became very worried for the safety of his family.

While he may have been fearful of their physical welfare, one thing he was never fearful of was his first son's spiritual condition, as Jonathan had made a profession of faith from a very early age. He was the sporty one, playing football, cricket, and tennis. However, his other son, Marcus, liked science, art, and music. Despite this, they were both involved in the activities of young people's work. Marcus was converted as a result of a dream he had of hell, and the concept of eternal separation. He said to me recently, that even now, when he thinks of hell, he could still fall on his knees in despair. Jonathan had asked to be baptised. James, knowing that his son was serious, felt that he should wait a little longer. Unknown to James, James' father who was now a member of a Methodist Church in Lancashire, was also coming under conviction of baptism, and had realised how important it was to be baptised. Knowing that his church didn't do full immersion baptism, he shared his conviction and the need for him to be baptised at the same time as Jonathan.

On the 14th of February in 1971, James had the rare privilege of baptising his father, and his son at the same time.

Baptism was becoming a common thing at West Street. Susan Barnes (now Susan Murdoch) recalls in the Spring of 1971, after the baptism of Norman Jones, how James did something very unusual. This is something that he hadn't done before (or since) and would eventually disagree with: the altar call. He had been wrestling with the idea all week, that at the end of the service he should make an appeal for people to come forward, asking them to do so and trust in the Lord for salvation, or for those interested in recommitting themselves to the Lord. Susan Barnes was one of those who came forward. Marcus also came forward, as well as twenty-two others. I also remember the occasion well, as a vivid childhood memory. We started to sing a hymn, and during the hymn, two people went forward, followed by another, and another. I remember thinking to myself, "what are all these people doing?" I remember looking at my father's face, at all these people who had come forward. A stunned look. As a direct result, 28 people were later baptised, and James' son Marcus was one of them.

Extraordinary blessings were taking place. But, what the congregation didn't know at that point was that their beloved pastor had been approached by another church from London, to consider being their Pastor. At first, James didn't consider it and dismissed it, but somehow he couldn't get this church out of his mind, and he felt that he should at least consider it. So, he agreed to preach there for the second time. Having spoken to all concerned, he reluctantly accepted the call to London. This did not appeal to Mum. She often made the prayer, "Lord, I will go anywhere except London." The decision was a hard one for James, one he had not taken lightly, but he announced his decision to leave after a Sunday night service. Again, with the memory of a young boy, I remember something being announced. There was stunned silence, then I saw people beginning to cry. I looked at my mum who was also weeping and I asked why everyone was crying. When she explained to me that it was because we were leaving, it hit me; I hadn't really grasped the concept until then. The ministry in Crewe had come to an end with tremendous blessing. My parents left the church on a high. Certainly, there were broken hearts, yet the whole family could look back with enormous gratitude to God for the blessing of seeing hard work, prayer, faithful ministry, and the fruit of their labour.

## 5

## BROADMEAD

WOODFORD GREEN IS AN AFFLUENT DISTRICT OF Redbridge, London. Historically, it was part of Essex, but it was absorbed into Greater London. It adjoins South Woodford, Woodford Wells, and Woodford Bridge. It has a history of well-known politicians who loved Woodford Green. Sylvia Pankhurst and Clement Atlee both lived there. Moreover, it was the constituency for which Sir Winston Churchill served from 1924 until he retired in 1964. A statue of him was unveiled on Woodford Green in 1959. He was undoubtedly one of James' heroes. Yet, that was all James knew about Woodford, except that Broadmead Baptist Church was there as well. The Broadmead years were mixed for James, there was blessing but also difficulties. Coming to London hit the family hard, especially Ailsa. Despite her prayers otherwise, she would spend the next 25 years in London. Jonathan and Marcus had the difficult time of making new friends and settling into a new secondary school. James himself missed the community life. In fact, it's fair to say that there were times when James thought that he had made a mistake in going to London. But it wasn't so much the change in going to London that hit James. The fact was, things were changing anyway. Things that James couldn't foresee, like for example, the rise of the Charismatic Movement in the late 70s and into the 1980s.

The church as a whole, was facing a change they hadn't faced before. A fellow LBC student, Clive Tyler, who was also a pastor, explained that, "Jim's plain speaking and lack of self-seeking meant that he and Ailsa struggled with the changing fashions of Christianity in the 1970s and in the years of spiritual declension that followed. Denominationalism, Church politics, and the required latitudinarianism didn't fit with their concern for a principled and holy ministry." There were also changes in society. If the 1960s were known as "the swinging 60s" (and its attendant rebelliousness), the 1970s were known more as a period of discontent. There was no way that James and Ailsa could know these changes were coming, and what's to say they wouldn't have faced the same conflicts if they had stayed in Crewe?

A problem for James was something Clive Tyler put simply as, "church politics." It was something James wasn't necessarily used to; no one likes problems, but at least the problems he had at Crewe were out in the open and exposed for what they were. James said this was the North-South divide literalised; he would say that Northerners were forth-right in their opinions, but it was a trait of Southerners to be hard to get through to, and that they wouldn't open up as much as Northerners did. Whether this is an accurate stereotype or not, it was one of the issues that faced James when he came to Broadmead; it all seemed too political.

The people, as a whole, were good people. Many of them had respectable jobs as city workers or bankers. Overall, most were "clever," but some were deceitful and scheming, which created an undercurrent that affected James' ministry. However, there was a lot of good at Broadmead. For instance, coming to London brought a new kind of ministry, with new opportunities. He could go to the Westminster Fraternal every month, not only to hear Dr Lloyd Jones, but also to be in the presence of many ministers. There were more opportunities for him to be involved in missionary work, which he loved, as many of these missionary societies were based in London. It wasn't very long before he was on the board of the Regions Beyond Missionary Union and involved with African Inland Mission. He wholeheartedly supported the London City Mission, with some of the workers attending the church. So, in that sense, his ministry did expand.

Broadmead was a fairly new church. It had a modern building, Sunday services were well attended, the youth work was good, but it was the Children's work that was especially successful. The reason for that was that Broadmead was an extension of Woodford which was a relatively new estate. Blocks of flats were built on the estate, which meant young people moving in. The church took advantage of this wonderful opportunity by having a nursery school there, using the hall as their premises. Since so many people wanted to get their children into the nursery school, the work became popular. All those volunteering had to be members of the church, which meant they had to be Christians. This perhaps explains why the Sunday School work was also popular.

The first pastor was Rev. Leslie Drew, who was inducted on the 2nd of November in 1963. He started a good work, and under his ministry the church membership grew from 48 to 92 people. The new building was ready for use and opened on the 28th of June in 1969. Yet, the following year Leslie Drew announced that he had accepted a call to Canada. This was a bit of a bombshell for the church because it was really flourishing. However, it was on the advice of Rev. Drew, that the church should find, pray, and seek for a Bible teacher who would build on the foundations he had helped to create. His view was that he had done the work of church planting, having set things up, but now it was time for the church to have a Bible teacher, who would build the work.

Rev. Dermot McDonald, the principal of LBC, who was vice principal to Ernest Kevan, was approached by the church, and he strongly urged the church to approach James Wood. On the 2nd of October in 1971, the induction service was conducted by Rev. John Waterman and Dermot MacDonald. Dr Lloyd Jones was approached but he was out of the country. According to Broadmead Church records, "numbers continued to grow, so that now 200 at the morning service was not unusual, and the midweek prayer meeting averaged an attendance of 50." What it doesn't record is that the evening services were also well attended, although it was not anywhere near the 200 mark like in Crewe. Despite things going well, there were two major problems that James was having to face.

The first problem was the old "Broadmeaders." They were there from the beginning; they were stubborn and set in their ways, and wanted to have things done as they were before. The second problem was James' reformed teaching. James' teaching ministry was well received, but what was not well received was his reformed thinking. As much as the work done by Rev. Drew had been good at the beginning, there wasn't any strong Bible teaching. This is no disrespect to Rev. Drew, because he started a good church and did a good job, but he later admitted to James that he knew this was a problem.

James had made his reformed position very clear from the start, to which the leadership responded with enthusiasm. But when this started being applied, overall, the old Broadmeaders didn't receive this teaching too kindly. James hadn't done anything to antagonise the situation. He hadn't made drastic changes. He still strongly supported the Nursery and the Sunday school. But, he felt as though the Youth Work was more about young people going to a club, rather than them learning about the Bible. This he felt needed to be addressed.

After addressing this, some of the young people left, causing the old Broadmeaders to become disgruntled. However, the youth work was re-focused and once again, it became very successful. James attributed the success to good youth leaders; some leaders were new, having replaced those who had gone into full time ministry. James had highlighted the importance of their time in the youth work, as it was a good training for them before going into ministry.

The problem for the old Broadmeaders was that

James' reformed preaching wasn't compromising enough, and they believed that James wasn't showing much care. Interestingly enough, they could never accuse James of a lack of pastoral care because he continued to visit people on a regular basis, to pray with them. They also came to accept that he was a clear Bible expositor, but they still couldn't accept the way the church was headed in the reformed position.

Another issue was that James couldn't allow things to continue if he felt they were unkind and unbiblical. So, he would confront them. However, this created a personality clash, and as a result, people took offence to what they called his "confrontational approach." As such, there was a power struggle, which unfortunately remained throughout James' ministry at Broadmead, and became a major thorn in his side, until it later escalated in his ministry.

In the meantime, positive things were taking place and there was great encouragement. The church continued to grow with more and more people joining; it was a real mixture of people from city workers, bankers, and professionals, to children from Barnardo's House, the children's home. Many people moving out of the East End came to join. For me, they were my favourites.

One couple that I do remember well was Mr. and Mrs. Latham, who lived in the Broadmead flats. Mr. Latham suffered terribly with asthma, a result of being gassed in the first world war. Mrs. Latham was from East Ham and had had a rough upbringing. Her father was a drunk who regularly beat up her mother. As a child, Mrs. Latham went to Sunday School shoe-less. The Sunday

School teachers were appalled, so they brought her some shoes. When she went home, her father took them off her and sold them, so that he could buy more alcohol with the money. I remember staying with Mr. and Mrs. Latham and enjoying it because they spoiled me rotten. But it was thanks to James's ministry that they were encouraged in their faith. James had the gift of being able to reach what would be called, the simple people of the world.

A personal blow to James' life in the early 70s was the passing of his mother. Her passing was sudden, but she always used to say, "sudden death, sudden glory." Fourteen months later, his father died as well. Ailsa started to go through periods of depression. Although Jonathan and Marcus were doing well academically, they hadn't really settled. My education was unsettling. I started school late because I was unable to talk until I was 5. I had attended two different junior schools while in Crewe. When the family moved to London there was no room for me in any of the local schools.

After 5 months, in early 1972, a school place became available. However, Jonathan had gained an interest in golf whilst on holiday in Scotland. One day, whilst practising with a 7-iron in the garden, he felt he had hit something at the end of his swing. On looking over his shoulder, he realised he had hit me right in the corner of my eye. This accident had the potential to make me blind, so I could not attend school for another 6 months. When finally I was able to return to school, they dropped me down a class because I was so far behind. When it was time for secondary school, James felt that the local comprehensive school would not be good enough given the additional challenges posed by my hearing loss and the disruption to my primary school years, so he sent me to a private school in Loughton. Still I made little progress, so James felt a school with smaller classes would be better, which did not exist other than boarding school.

The local authority agreed to fund my place, and so, in 1975, James sent me to boarding school, Brickwall House, in Northiam, East Sussex. One consequence of this was that I received no Christian teaching, only on holidays or selected weekends, which is why I drifted away from the Lord. For James, the waywardness of his son was an added burden, with constant phone calls to report bad behaviour, of running away from school only to be returned by police, and being accident prone. However, this was another ministry that James entered, a greater understanding of those whose children go astray.

Yet, despite James' personal worries, he kept the church's vision focused. In the middle of the 1970s, he introduced eldership. Some didn't like this because they wanted to be elders themselves. Dick Little, who was involved in the early days of the work of Broadmead, became an elder. Then Chris Frohwein, a London city missionary, who joined the church in 1974, was also introduced as an elder. Chris, who remained a good friend to James until his dying days, was working amongst Eastern European Seamen in the London docks, and became a missionary to London's underground workers. With this, there grew a greater interest in the work of missionaries.

Janet Helens, following her training as a nurse, went

to Peru with Regions Beyond Missionary Union (RBMU). She went to work with the Quechuan Indians in 1972. This is where James met Geoff Larcombe, the director of RBMU, who invited James to join the mission's home board. With this positive outlook on missionary work, the church at Broadmead became missionary-minded. James later went into the heart of Zaire with RBMU to see the work of missionaries stationed there. James introduced to the church two missionaries whom he supported and whom the church from Crewe supported, Valerie Hamilton and Roland, as well as Jean Knight, who worked with Mission Aviation Fellowship in Tanzania.

Roland went to West Street while training at Crewe as an engineer with Rolls Royce. Incredibly, his sister lived in Woodford, so he transferred his membership to Broadmead. With a steady flow of conversions, and members increasing, to the point where chairs had to be put out in the entrance lobby, there was a blessed period. Certain men in the church felt called to ministry, including Trevor Reynolds, a qualified solicitor who went to Trinity College, Bristol and became an assistant Pastor in Wales. Ray Tibbs worked as Extension Secretary for the Sudan United Mission, and was one of the first students at London Theological Seminary, later to become a Pastor in Ramsey, Cambridgeshire. In 1982, Bob Penhearow went to the Baptist seminary in Toronto, then received a calling to be Pastor in Canada. Keith Ferdinando went to London Bible College and then went to East Africa. Finally, Jonathan Wood in 1985, went to be an assistant Pastor to Herbert Carson in Leicester. It truly was a time of blessing.

Unfortunately, things started to turn sour when James wanted Paul Doye to become an elder. Paul had been a member at Broadmead long before James's arrival, and he was incredibly supportive to James' ministry. When James introduced Paul to be an elder, this was not accepted by four men who were deacons: the church secretary, the next day, handed in his resignation, throwing all the books on the table of James' study desk. The treasurer voiced his opinion strongly in opposition. Another man, who was quite scheming, also voiced his opposition to James privately, and was very clearly the ringleader in what was to follow. A fourth deacon also resigned, but I don't think he knew what he had resigned for.

A church meeting was called which resulted in a very heated discussion. The former treasurer shouted down another member, while the former church secretary claimed that James was not being honest. Later, when Paul Doye becoming an elder was up for vote, it was rejected, which left a sour taste and changed the atmosphere. An undercurrent filled the church, and the church then became divided. The problem was that James was always viewed as being defensive. I remember for example, after one church meeting, the ringleader going up to James with his back to the people saying, "let me shake your hand pastor, despite that unforgivable remark you made earlier on." James replied, and people immediately thought they were arguing. The pettiness went on, and James became exhausted. On top of this, were the Charismatic issues of the 80s, and the mission campaigns which were used against James' ministry. In

1985, James resigned. This caused a split, with supporters of James' ministry leaving to worship elsewhere.

A very sad chapter ended for James' ministry; clearly church politics did not suit him. However, James had reached a peak, with so many people throughout his time at Broadmead entering full-time Christian ministry. In addition to those previously mentioned, Steven Ball went to work for Child Evangelism Fellowship, Helen Derchez went to Niger with Africa Inland Mission, Carol Fischer went to Kenya with Africa Inland Mission, Martin Hull also attended LTS and went on to be a pastor in Grove Hill, David Morgan became a pastor, Tim Hull went to work for the London City Mission and Leon and Susan Thomas later went as missionaries to Cambodia, all of which gave James great joy. Even his youngest son, Timothy, who had finally been converted in 1982, went to LTS between 1986 and 1988, and went on to pastor in Wigmore, Kent, where I continue to the present day.

# 6

## AFRICA

A GROUP OF ABOUT 60, THAT HAD LEFT BROADMEAD, started meeting at Paul Doye's home and then in a public room at the bottom of a block of flats known as Tamar Square. It was assumed by some that James would continue to be the Pastor. That was not James' position, nor was it the position of everyone else. James, by then, had been asked by Africa Inland Mission if he would consider going to a Bible college in Kenya to be a lecturer. James was thrilled by this. The breakaway group had named themselves as Woodford Evangelical Church, and they supported his going to Kenya, although some were disappointed by his decision. Some had hoped that he would go to Kenya for a year and then come back and continue as Pastor, but James did not think this, nor did he ever agree to it. He did want to maintain close connection with Woodford but did not believe that he should be the Pastor.

The time had come for James to go to Kenya with Ailsa. James had already been to Kenya, as well as Zaire, and had already been in touch with a Pastor in Kenya by the name of Keith Underhill, as well as John Langat, and Lawrence Bomett. While there, he was able to go and see Keith and Margaret Ferdinando, and even spent Christmas with them. James loved his time in Kenya and gained a great understanding of the African Church. He saw that while many of these men in college were keen, enthusiastic followers of Christ, there was a great need for them to be trained. He saw that African preachers were very good story tellers but were not expounding the scriptures as they should. He then took it upon himself to train and teach these men the importance of reading good, theological books, and how to expound the scriptures. He rose to the occasion because the students responded well.

Ailsa, in the meantime, had the pleasure of giving talks to the student's wives. Ailsa's stay, however, was cut short when, after 6 months, she had to go home due to illness. James stayed for another 3 months, and I believe he also went to Zaire, to visit Robert and Dorothy Dear.

When he returned to England, he did preach at Woodford Evangelical Church, but there was a strange quietness from the leaders. James made it easier for them and declined to be Pastor. That was fine for James as he did not assume that he would be offered the job as Pastor when he returned, but the leaders at Woodford had been vague with him about his future at the church.

WEC is now under the leadership of Jon Drane, a good, godly man, and the church meets at Prospect Road. James visited a couple of times.

# 7

## WALTHAMSTOW CENTRAL BAPTIST CHURCH

AFTER THIS, JAMES HAD A BREAK FROM THE MINISTRY. HE continued to preach up and down the country, but it would be fair to say that he was getting older and more tired each day. He took on a job working for a wedding company in Epping. Central Baptist Church in Walthamstow then came knocking at his door, with whom there was a connection through Barbara Collins, who was working for Africa Inland Mission and later went as a missionary to the Comores. The church had just come through a trying period where some folk had left due to charismatic issues. They felt that they needed not just a man that could preach but a man who showed pastoral care. I know that there was a great deal of reluctance on James' part to go there, not just because he was despondent with the way that churches were going, but because he was tired of the work. Yet, the calling was so compelling, that he accepted, the induction service being led by Leith Samuel and Herbert Carson.

By now, two of his sons had begun their ministries,

whilst Marcus had followed in his paternal grandfather's footsteps, becoming a dental surgeon. I began my ministry at Wigmore Evangelical Free Church in Kent in November of 1990, and Jonathan, having completed his time as assistant at Knighton Free Church in Leicester, began a new ministry in Musselburgh Baptist Church, just outside of Edinburgh in 1993. In the first months of my ministry, there was a coup to remove me from the pastorate. This alarmed my dad, as it would any good father; nevertheless, the issue was solved by removing the troublemakers.

Dad had always taught me to face trials head-on, and this was the same for him at Walthamstow where the treasurer had been ruling the church with an iron fist. He was acting in a very controlling way with the accounts; he had the say where the money went and even if he had been told by the deacons, he wouldn't allow money to be spent on things he didn't want. This became a problem for James, and he decided that he had to take on this bully. This man was consequently removed from his office as treasurer. The church then pressed ahead, and it was a very happy church.

I believe that James and Ailsa were happy there. They loved the fact that Walthamstow was East London, and they loved the honesty of East Enders. They also loved the fact that Walthamstow was very multi-cultural, and there were many Africans and Asians in attendance. I noticed a slight change of style in James' preaching, where he preached more on passages than he did individual verses.

The church grew into a loving and caring fellowship,

until James retired in 1998. Again, James had the thrill of one of his members going into ministry when Jon Davies later accepted a call to the pastorate of Cromer Baptist Church in Norfolk.

## 8

## PREACHING

JAMES TOOK ON THE MINISTRY WITH A GREAT DEAL OF seriousness. That's not to say that he was faultless. Indeed, by his own admission, he made mistakes. Yet, James felt that if ministry was entered into recklessly or carelessly, the consequences would be enormous. No doubt, the conviction of his calling came to him independently by the work of the Holy Spirit, yet he was influenced by the spiritual leaders of the day, Lloyd-Jones and Ernest Kevan.

Ernest Kevan was worried about the young men in his day, about the different challenges that lay ahead for them. He foresaw the changes and therefore, the challenges that lay ahead for the ministry. He foresaw the gospel being watered-down, an increase of shallow teaching, and the threat of increased liberalism. Ernest Kevan came to preach for James while in Crewe. In the afternoon, we would all go to Sunday School while Ernest Kevan stayed behind with my Granny, who came to stay with us for the weekend. He told her of his fear for the

young men in the ministry. It wasn't just the change in
the ministry that bothered Ernest Kevan, but it was the
morals of the day. For example, issues arose that the
church hadn't really had to deal with before, such as
divorce and remarriage. In fact, my father remembers
Ernest giving a lecture on marriage, divorce, and remarriage, whether this was permitted in the scriptures or not,
saying, "brethren, I don't want to be dogmatic on this
subject, because I have changed my mind on the issue at
least 5 times."

It was perhaps out of Ernest Kevan's concern for his
students that he kept in touch with all of them, after they
had left LBC. James always appreciated the letters he
received of warmth and encouragement.

As much as Ernest Kevan was a great influence on
James, there was an even closer relationship between
James and Lloyd-Jones. James did not intend to downplay
his relationship with Ernest Kevan in any way; he simply
felt a warmer relationship with Lloyd-Jones. It's fair to say
that Lloyd-Jones was a Pastor's Pastor. The fact is, Lloyd-
Jones had a powerful ministry in his day. After a powerful
ministry in Wales, he was called to Westminster Chapel
where he was first the associate minister to Campbell
Morgan, and when he retired, then took over the
ministry. During the war years, London was packed with
foreign soldiers, and people from the commonwealth
countries, as well as America. Soldiers from Europe and
all over the world came to hear him preach. At the end of
the war, the ministry at Westminster Chapel had a reputation not seen in London since the days of Spurgeon.
Lloyd-Jones' ministry continued throughout the 50s and

60s, changing the evangelical scene. The reason for this was the way that Dr Lloyd Jones emphasised preaching and its importance. He emphasised the centrality of Biblical preaching calling it, "fire with logic." He understood preaching as "the mind, to the heart, to activate the will." This of course, was the pattern that James aimed at with his ministry.

Of course, Dr Lloyd Jones was a very popular man, but he was also very humble and very caring. He did not see himself as a cut above the rest, and he made time for every pastor. He was a good example for all preachers to follow. He wanted to encourage all men in the ministry as much as he could, and this extended also to their wives and families. James very much put himself under his wise counsel and advice in his own ministry. He also followed the Dr Lloyd Jones principle of expository preaching - preaching that expands a biblical text beyond its face value.

James' seriousness in the ministry was because he had a standard. The standard that he set was that all preaching should be Christ-exalting and Christ-uplifting. Therefore, he believed that a preacher should do away with anything that might only draw attention to himself. Just as James had high regard for the ministry, there was a sense in which he expected the same from the people. I remember for example, that during the days of Broadmead, when meeting in the vestry with the deacons and elders, he would lead the procession out of the vestry, then walk to the pulpit and sit down. The deacons and elders would go to their own seats, and after a moment when he would say a quick prayer to himself, as soon as he stood up, the whole congregation would also stand up. This to him, was the call to worship. This was the cut-off point, where people knew now that the time for talking should stop so that they could focus on worship.

Anything less than that, he saw as flippant. He couldn't stand flippancy in worship. This, to him, was also why he believed that the man in the pulpit should lead the congregation with a dress code of suit and tie. He struggled with the modern approach of ministers not wearing a tie. James very much followed the, "hymn sandwich," pattern, a traditional format to a service.

When it came to the sermon, he made the text clear from the beginning and where the text was going to take them. His notes were shorthand, 4 sides of A5. If you were to look at the notes, the only thing most people would be able to follow would be the headings. Anything other than that, you would have had to work hard to understand.

His sermons were exceedingly well structured and as I have listened to them over the years, I have made several observations. Firstly, his sermons were all theological; he always preached directly from the text. The theological knowledge that he had was drawn out of his sermons, so much so, that as you listened it was a sermon full of simple and understandable theology. He would be pleased if he knew someone had said this about his sermons, as he strongly believed people should be able to understand the scriptures as much as possible. He believed that theology, once it was applied, would lead to a response. He didn't have a lot of time for preaching that focused on being practical, rather he believed that theology would make a person practical.

Secondly, it was exposition. It has been noted that his years at Broadmead were more of a teaching ministry. In that sense, he had no fear of exposition and to be known for having a teaching ministry. He saw it as a failure amongst some preachers, especially when he went to Africa, that there was a lack of emphasis on teaching. He saw this as an opportunity to explain this to many of the Africans. He understood expository preaching as a form of preaching that outlines the meaning of the text or passage of scripture, and saw to it that you expand the text as much as possible. In this way, he believed you imparted knowledge.

Thirdly, he believed that discipline was crucial. Not only in preparation but also in the delivery of the sermon. He had little tolerance for unnecessary long-windedness, and he had a problem with what he termed 'Bible rambling' while in Africa. This is when a person expands a text by using a concordance. In this area, he was critical, especially when young men first began and were far too long. As far as he was concerned, a young man starting out should be disciplined to preach for half an hour, no longer.

Fourthly, the use of English language was important to him. One of James' heroes was William Tyndale. For him, it wasn't just the fact that he translated the Bible from the Hebrew and Greek to English, nor not that he defied the King, but it was his use of the English language. As much as he understood that this was an area that some may struggle with, he also believed that it should be corrected when necessary. For instance, I remember when he took me aside once and said, "the English language is one of the richest languages in the world. What one language can explain in one word, the English language can explain in five, so it's extremely important to have a good vocabulary." James' use of English was appealing. He had certain favourite phrases like, "therefore," which kept the flow. It was also important to him to speak clearly with good English grammar.

Fifthly, he was bold. He was bold not just in that he was unafraid to spell it out, as it was. But, in that he never shied away from depth. He once said to me that you should never, "underestimate the hearer." In other words, you don't adjust because you are preaching to a bunch of intellectuals or preaching to the less well-educated or knowledgeable. Rather, you present the truth as it is, in a simple way, equally, for everyone to understand, regardless of their academic status. When he announced his topic at the beginning of the sermon, I remember a couple of times thinking that they sounded a bit heavy, for example, "How Christian is the Roman Catholic Church?" or, "What do we mean by justification by faith alone?" But for James, these were fundamentals, and therefore, the people should know this, and as long as it was presented in a simple way, for him it should be boldly presented.

Sixthly, he was engaging. In his sermons, James would always engage with the people. By delivering a sermon, a preacher communicates their message for people to hear. The danger for the preacher, is when they realise they may be losing the concentration of people, and so, it's easy to use too many side-track methods to engage people such as illustrations or humour. For James, too much humour draws attention to the speaker, and the same goes for too many illustrations. Not that James was against using either of these methods, because he would use them himself, though he mainly used illustrations from scripture. This was his way of saying, "let scripture speak for itself." In fact, I remember someone saying to me that he noticed that James didn't have to use illustrations because he was so Bible based that they remained focused because they were, "afraid of missing something that he says."

Penultimately, his sermons were passionate. James was critical of those who lacked passion. He believed that preaching with passion was showing belief in what you were preaching. He felt that a passionless sermon was cold, lifeless, and dull. He also believed that you could preach with passion without getting emotional. He said that preaching should be passionate but controlled, so as not to come across as overly emotional.

Finally, was his application. This was possibly one of his greatest strengths. He said to me that, "application is one of the most important aspects in any sermon." He said that it was pointless preaching a sermon without application. He once heard a man give what he said was a good sermon, but said that he spoilt it all by not applying the message. Application is crucial because by presenting your case to the people, you are challenging them with the message by asking, "what are you doing about this to maintain your walk with the Lord?" He said to me that, "you need to apply the message as much as possible. You can get away with a bad sermon by applying the message." His sermons had a lasting effect.

There will always be sermons that people will remember and will always stay with them. Sermons are meant to have a long-term effect on you, and they will if accompanied by the power of the holy spirit. I can recall many times when people have come up to me and said, "I remember when your father preached a series on 1 Corinthians, Isaiah, James, John, Ephesians." A lady once said to me that after hearing James, she would often wonder if, at the time, it had affected her. But she said that, "as the week went on," she could remember everything that he had said that Sunday. She explained, "there were times when I listened to the preacher and it affected me at the time but come the end of the day, I had forgotten what they had said. Whereas with your father, it stayed with me the whole week, until the next one."

A moving story I've never forgotten, is of a woman that was given three months to live. During that period, she laid out all the sermon notes that she had taken from James' sermons, and with her Bible, she went through them all. There's one sermon I never forget because it wasn't just that the sermon itself that was powerful at the time, but it was the response after. After he closed the service in prayer and walked down from the pulpit, no one moved. This was just after he preached from John 14. 30-31. His sermons were always Christ-centred; his favourite phrase was always, the "Lamb of God." If his sermons were from the Old Testament, he always made sure that Christ was brought up. If it was a teaching element, he still brought Christ into it. When he preached the gospel, evangelistically he brought Christ in. Christ was the need, the source, the supply, the giver, and the power. Anything less than this, he would say, was not a sermon.

The number of letters and emails that were sent to me after his departure, centred on that theme, that James Wood showed people Christ.

Much more could be said about the ministry of sermons, such as mannerism, style, gesture, and what he didn't like to see in the pulpit, his pet peeve being preaching with your hands in your pockets. But these are trivial compared to the big things, like preaching the whole counsel of God. This James did - faithfully, diligently, and willingly, obeying the charge that Paul gave to Timothy, "Preach the word, out of season and in season."

*James and Ailsa's courtship*

*80th Birthday celebrations at the beach hut, Frinton,*
*May 2011.*

*James (right) and Peter with their father.*

*James in his youth.*

*James with a MKIV Centurion Tank.*

*James was a proficient rider.*

*James & Ailsa's wedding day, 28th July 1956.*

*With James' parents (left) and Ailsa's father and stepmother (right).*

*James (right) with his father and Peter on Peter's*
*wedding day.*

*A family group photo during the Crewe years.*

*James at his induction at Central Baptist Church, Walthamstow.*

*James enjoying his hobby making model trains.*

*James in Africa.*

*A family group with sons, daughters in law and grandchildren in 2009.*

*With his beloved Labrador, Chloe.*

*James and Alisa c.2013.*

*With their sons, shortly before Ailsa was called home in 2014.*

*James with all 8 grandchildren, their spouses and a great granddaughter in 2018.*

# 9

# HOME LIFE

IF I HAVE PORTRAYED MY FATHER AS FAULTLESS, THIS IS A chapter where I may have to let him down. He was a workaholic, and in many ways his work came first. Still, he was a good father, a good husband, and a good family man, although sometimes his work affected his family life. Meetings, seeing people, and getting work done came first. This came from his sense of calling. Many times, our dinner would be interrupted by a phone call, meaning he would leave the family and his dinner to answer. Mum would then put his dinner in the oven, to keep warm.

As a father, he was very strict. Sometimes he could be severe, not in an abusive manner, but it was often in a spur of the moment. For example, I remember one Sunday evening play fighting with one of my brothers, and we accidentally knocked over a vase. He came racing over and dragged us into his study to give us a good ticking off. He wouldn't tolerate any silliness from us and his methods of discipline would today be seen not only as extreme but unthinkable. Yet, for us to toe the line was important to him, not just because he had to be seen as having disciplined children, but also for our own sakes.

As parents, they were fair, reasonable, and loving, but they could be very strict disciplinarians, having no hesitation in using methods which would not be acceptable nowadays. The Proverb writer says, in 22. 6, "Train a child the way they should go and not the way they want to go." We, as children, received lots of smacks. Maybe we needed them, but sometimes the discipline was perhaps overly harsh. This sometimes made Dad out to be scary at the time, and we would dread his homecoming. Yet, I look back with thankfulness and say, "it didn't do me any harm." I remember doing something at school, which resulted in me getting the cane. With shame, I had to face my parents. We sat in the front room and I feared the worst. But he was calm, in control and very spiritual. He kept saying, "you know that the blood of Jesus Christ washes us of all our sins." I said, "absolutely." Then he said, "let's pray" calmly followed by, "bend down." And of course, out came the belt. He told me that it was going to hurt him more than me, and I didn't protest or resist, but I did scream at the pain. It hurt, but I never did it again.

I don't believe Dad did it because he was concerned for his reputation, nor just to keep the words Paul said to Timothy, "how can an elder lead a flock when he can't manage his family?" He did it because he didn't like unruliness, and because he loved us, saying that it was part and parcel of being a pastor's kid. There was a sense in which you couldn't win. I'm not being critical, but I believe Dad was being cautious with his children and did not want to be seen as favouring them. For example, it seemed he would rarely choose us if we had put our hands up during the children's talk. This carried on into my calling. He did not want to be seen as the one pushing it, he wanted to ensure that it was the other way round. When the expectations of being a pastor's kid were placed upon us by the community, even though he understood our situation, he wouldn't excessively support us because, for him, that was simply part of the calling.

He was always fair, sometimes to the extent that it surprised you. When you thought you were in serious trouble, you would find that you were not. I recall a time when I was suspended at school. I knew I was in serious trouble, and when I met with him at the station, I immediately told him I was sorry, but he said, "I'll talk to you in the morning." I was surprised at his belief in my version of events, and what he portrayed as unfairness. About 30 other boys were involved in what I did, and he couldn't understand why I was the only one who was sanctioned.

Family devotions were always at the top of the agenda. They would also read out stories to us, like "Pilgrim's Progress," "John Newton's Life," Martin Luther, and famous missionaries. They encouraged us to read the magazine published monthly by "Open Doors," about persecuted Christians behind the Iron Curtain. We always went to church, and never missed church unless there was an illness. TV on Sundays was not allowed. We attended Sunday Services, Youth Clubs, and went to Christian Youth Camps. Aside from the missionaries who came to stay with us, we also had a Great Aunt who had been a missionary in India for over 50 years, serving with the Bible Missionary Medical Fellowship (BMMF). We loved to hear her stories. We were privileged, as many missionaries came to stay with us, as well as Preachers and Christians who had escaped persecution. Our house always seemed to welcome visitors.

As a Pastor's child, I was not fully aware of the problems that were going on in church life. That is because our parents protected us from that. They wouldn't talk about these things in the hearing of little ears. As the child of a Pastor, expectations for good behaviour were high. Comments like, "and he's the Pastor's son," didn't help matters. But expectations were also high from our parents. As a teenager. I was sitting in the back row, with a few others, fidgeting and talking, when my father stopped the sermon, flicked his fingers at me and said, "Timothy, will you please be quiet!" I froze and didn't dare move once during the sermon. That affected the whole congregation, who also didn't dare move!

AT HOME, he wasn't the most relaxed person. He always had to be doing something. He was a man with many hobbies; if he wasn't working, he would be engaged in one or other of them. Monday was usually his day off. If he wasn't going to the Westminster Fellowship – which was on a Monday – he was making his model trains or planes. He would spend hours making them. He loved art, especially oil painting. He and Marcus would sometimes go away on trips to paint together. His loft was full of paintings which he had created. He was a keen gardener and carpenter and loved doing DIY projects. He was very aware of current affairs, where his reading of the paper came second only to his Bible and devotions. He was forthright in his political opinions and as much as he would express them to his family, he would never impose them on people and certainly never talk about them from the pulpit. As far as he was concerned, you should leave politics out of the pulpit. He always argued that politics divides, whereas the gospel should build bridges. He was a Tory, but he had a great concern for social justice. His eyes were opened to this in his early days in London, but especially in Crewe. He saw poverty and lived with the poor, but he also saw how political power abused the system, and he hated that.

He loved to read history, especially history concerning the church. His spiritual heroes were Martin Luther, John Calvin, Thomas Watson, William Tyndale, Charles Spurgeon, and Dr Martyn Lloyd-Jones. He also had great admiration for Oliver Cromwell, who he argued was the champion for present day democracy. He loved the Puritans and their works. He loved the Pilgrim Fathers and would tell me the story about the Mayflower. With his knowledge of boats, he would tell me how the Mayflower was made for the treacherous waters of the Atlantic. His reading was mainly of theological books, Church history, and history books, especially military history. He was a great admirer of William Shakespeare, mainly because of his love for the English language. For him, the quality of the writing was equally important to the content. For example, when the Harry Potter books came out, he wanted to know what all the fuss was about. So, he started to read it, and his remark was: "this is ever so well written." His grandson Thomas is an author, and James used to comment more on the quality of his English than the content of his books.

His love for gardening would leave him spending many hours in the garden, especially when he retired. Nothing annoyed him more than when we, as boys, would play football in the garden and knock the ball onto his plants. My parents were incredibly loving and supportive, always encouraging in whatever hobbies or passions we had. But our Dad didn't show a significant interest in the things we liked unless he liked them too. When I was on a football team, I would ask him to come watch me, but I don't actually remember him coming to watch me at all. Yet, if he liked something you were doing, he would respond to it well: to Jonathan's theological interest as a young man, to Marcus' love for oil painting, to my love of horse riding and history. In fact, when he had learnt I had taken up horse riding at boarding school, he was fascinated; we used to speak for ages about horses and history.

Everyone who knew James well, will tell you what a great sense of humour he had. Because of the nature of his job, and his appearance of seriousness, this was misunderstood. However, being such a good storyteller, he would go through every detail in a humorous way. Because of his great acting ability, he could keep a straight face while everyone was laughing, and sometimes you didn't know if he was annoyed or if he was simply just keeping a straight face.

I remember an occasion when a woman in the Church of Broadmead asked if she could do a solo. He didn't want her to, because he didn't believe that solos were helpful in a worship service. However, on this one occasion at the very beginning of his ministry in Woodford, he allowed it to happen, and his point was proved. From the moment that she started, the woman couldn't hit the right note, and the whole congregation was on the floor laughing, but somehow, he managed to keep a straight face.

Of course, there were times when he let his guard down and sometimes, he would be wheezing so much you would begin to worry about how hard he was laughing!

He didn't play any musical instruments, yet he loved music, mainly classical music, especially Mozart, Handel, and Bach. If I had lost an LP, there would be no point looking in Dad's LP cupboard, because it was full of classical music. And yes, steam train LPs as well! On a Sunday evening, after a busy day of preaching, Dad would be found at 9pm sitting in the lounge listening to 'Your Hundred Best Tunes' on Radio 2, and woe betide anyone who interrupted!

He didn't watch much TV, only the news. He liked classical dramas and all the Charles Dickens TV productions. He also enjoyed some older comedy programmes like "Dad's Army," "Morecambe and Wise," "It Ain't Half Hot Mum," "Some Mothers Do Have Them," and "Only Fools and Horses." He loved watching the Rugby, especially the Home Nations and World Cup. For many, this may be surprising, but he also liked watching boxing, although many times I would hear him say, "stop the fight." He didn't like football as much; the modern game irritated him, and he preferred the old fashioned game with the likes of Stanley Matthews, Bobby Charlton and Bobby Moore. However, he would watch the World Cup and European Championships. In fact, he went to watch a World Cup game in 1966 at Goodison Park and went with Jonathan to the FA Cup Final in 1968 with tickets provided by his father in law. But on the whole football and modern footballers did not impress him. Amusingly, he was once conducting a funeral service at the crematorium in Manor Park, East London, when someone excitedly told him that David Beckham was one of the mourners. This would have been just as Mr Beckham's footballing career was gathering momentum, but my Dad's response was "who's he?" much to the consternation of his sons and grandsons who would have loved to shake the hand of David Beckham as Dad did! At least we are assured that David Beckham has heard the gospel, because James would not have let such an opportunity go! And James was amused that David left in his impressive Porsche which had been parked next to his own battered old Ford Escort!

I think it's fair to say that he relaxed more with his family while on holidays. We had lots of holidays which were cheap and cheerful. We didn't know that at the time, and we didn't need to know because they were still enjoyable. We would mostly go camping in places like Scotland, Wales, and Cornwall. At times, we went to Austria, Germany, and France but his favourite destination of all was the Lake District. There was a time when we had a cottage there, near the Tarn Hows. I remember one year, during his sabbatical, we stayed there, and when the lake froze we skated on it for hours.

As I mentioned, he was a very disciplined man and couldn't stand slacking. He would wake up early in the morning, and he would let the household know! He expected the household to have the same discipline: tidy bedrooms and always being punctual for family events. As a very punctual man himself, he would often be frustrated with Mum, because of her lack of urgency.

But the overriding quality that he had was that he was a leader. He wasn't dictatorial, he just took the lead. When a decision was made, that was it; this was especially true in our prayer devotions as a family. Always after dinner, the Bible came out, followed by prayers. He had a rota showing whose turn it was to read and whose turn it was to pray. He would always explain the Bible reading. This was motivated by the fact that in his private time, he was a man of prayer, and made time for prayer. In his last years while he was on his own, he was constantly praying. This made it easy for him because he struggled with prayer in his early life.

I thank God that he was a man of prayer. I recall one occasion, before I was converted, walking into his bedroom without knocking on the door, and he was on his knees making this prayer that I can only assume was about me: "Lord, save him, save him, he has drifted away from you, and only you can bring him to yourself." I have often used that as an illustration of how Jesus prays for us all, just as an earthly father pleads on behalf of his children, how much more does Jesus plead on our behalf?

His prayer was answered when in the June of 1982, I surrendered my life to Christ, while in a police cell, remembering all the things my parents told me as a child, with Biblical stories and truths. For this, I thank God for the father and mother I had.

## 10

## A WAYWARD SON

I HAVE A GREAT DEAL OF RELUCTANCE WRITING THIS chapter. There are things I have done that have caused me both a great deal of shame and a lot of grief. I am also aware that this book is a tribute to James and therefore, should be focused on him. However, there are two reasons why I refer to my testimony. One, because this became another ministry that James had, encouraging parents with wayward children. Even to this day, people still speak to me about the encouragement James gave them. He would tell them to keep bringing this matter to the Lord, and then he would refer to the experience he had with me. But there is a second reason why I speak about his prodigal son who returned. Unknown to me, he went through a stage where he seriously considered giving up the ministry. He confided in my older brother and thought long and hard about whether he should continue in his ministry.

I think it's best to first give you the backstory of my conversion and then put together various pieces of advice he gave to parents who had wayward children. The trouble with some testimonies, is that they tend to justify the past, rather than justify God and his work of salvation. Under these circumstances, I wish to refer to just a bit of the past to understand the personal trials which James had to endure while facing the challenges of the ministry at the same time.

1962 was a very difficult time for James and Ailsa. The manse was small, church life hadn't really taken off, and Ailsa had had a miscarriage. Due to her blood type, she was advised against having any more children. So, it came as no surprise that when I was born, there were complications. I was born completely jaundiced and had severe breathing difficulties. This meant I had to have a blood transfusion. The only problem was, the senior doctor was away, and the responsibility was left to the junior doctor. By his admission, he was left with no choice but to carry out the blood transfusion, during which my heart stopped beating. This meant having to perform defibrillation, which restored my life, but came with consequences. While this was all taking place, James was about to enter the pulpit, when a policeman came into the vestry and advised him not to preach but instead, go to the hospital. He didn't take the advice and carried on preaching. Meanwhile, a nurse was about to take me to a Priest to say the rites over me. When Ailsa heard this, she used all her strength and was adamant this should not happen.

After 2-3 weeks in hospital, I arrived in my new home. As I grew, my parents noticed that I wasn't responding well when they called me and considered the possibility that I was deaf. At the age of 5, after having tests, the audiology proved that I had a hearing deficiency, probably as a result of the defibrillation carried out by a doctor who was not adequately trained in the use of such a technique on an infant. It came to the point that I was encouraged to wear hearing aids, as the tests showed that I had 70% hearing loss in my right ear and 30% hearing loss in my left ear. As a child, I refused to wear a hearing aid, as it felt uncomfortable at the time. The teachers were surprised that despite some obvious difficulty, I was keeping up. They soon discovered that I had learnt the art of lip reading. The hearing specialist suggested that if the hearing aids were uncomfortable, they should let me continue to progress with lip reading. Growing up with this difficulty, I was always aware of how my parents were concerned, even fearful, of me crossing the road, as they were worried I might not hear a vehicle.

As parents, it was rare for our parents to interfere with school. They were supportive of schools, always attending parents' evenings and other school activities. I was disciplined several times and it would be of no use to protest my innocence. But there was one time when James felt that the school had crossed the line and he objected to my PE teacher who was in the Royal Air Force. Although this teacher had left, he continued to train Alsatian dogs for the RAF. For one of my PE lessons, he took us out on to the sports field and put a dog training sleeve on our arms. He made us run up the field and then let the dog run free, and the dog would then chase and jump onto our sleeve pad. When it was my turn, I was terrified, as I watched this Alsatian dog chase me with his mouth wide open, tongue hanging out of his mouth, salvia dripping and teeth as wild as a wolf. When he caught up with me, I fell onto the ground. I let go of the arm pad where he started to rip it apart, but then he saw me, he jumped on me and bit me. By this time, the PE instructor had run over to me, pulled back the dog and started to scold me for letting go of the arm pad. After school, I reported this to my parents, and they took me to the doctor, who gave me a tetanus injection. This was a step too far for my father who went to the school and complained. We never saw the PE teacher again. I became an unexpected hero of the school, where it was rumoured that "Woody's" dad got rid of him. Years later, I asked Dad about the incident and he told me that when he went to the school, they made it clear to him that this was just one of the several things for which the teacher was under investigation.

When I turned 13, a big change took place, as mentioned previously. My parents didn't think I was doing well at school. The classes were too big, and I wasn't hearing well. They felt it was best that I sit in small classes. The only place that accommodated smaller classes was boarding school. I was alarmed at this and had no desire to go. Boarding school was tough, and it was where I learnt the first life lesson: look after yourself. The plus side was that you learnt independence quicker and that it gave you a certain amount of self-belief. However, this too came at a cost, where you risked becoming aggressive and very competitive.

Whilst I didn't enjoy boarding school, I wasn't completely unhappy there. The main problem was that you couldn't share the bad days and the good days with your parents. If anything went wrong, you couldn't speak to them about it. Not only that, but my spiritual life took a beating. I only ever went to church on certain weekends and holidays. My parents noticed this change in my life, where I was losing all interest in spiritual things. I ran away from school once, in my socks having had my shoes confiscated. This led to my first encounter with the police, who were waiting for me at the train station to take me back to school. This got me into serious trouble with the school and with my father. I learnt to smoke at school, and listened to coarse jokes; my language was no better. An incident at school that took place involved me being suspended, at which point my parents thought it was best to take me out of school. When I left school, things didn't improve. I no longer went to church, I cared very little for spiritual things, and I became marked by the local police.

I then joined a gang; we roamed the streets, getting up to no good. Living in London gave us opportunities to attend night clubs, concerts, football matches, and other activities. Late nights became frequent and sometimes I didn't come home, causing my parents more worry. I would follow the latest fashion trends to be part of the in-crowd. I was a "skinhead" and then a "mod" with my own scooter. Street fights became a regular thing, especially after late night drinking. On top of coming home in a drunken state, I would be covered in bruises and cuts, prompting my father to ask what happened to me? Football hooliganism was another thing I got caught up in. The 70s and 80s were bad decades for football hooliganism, so Mrs. Thatcher set up a committee to deal with it. This was spearheaded by Douglas Hurd, the home secretary at the time.

I used to look forward to those Saturdays, where I travelled to the West Ham ground or to away games. Football matches were not safe places, especially if you tried to enter the "away fans" area. Once I did this, and a fight spilled over, causing a policeman to swing his baton at me, whacking my neck. This caused me to stumble, and before I knew it, I was at the bottom of a stampede. When I returned home, I was met with despairing looks from my parents.

In fact, my first adult encounter with the police was at West Ham's Football ground, Upton Park. I was arrested for insulting behaviour and frog-marched away by two police officers, taken into what looked like a police control room, followed by handcuffs behind my back, and was escorted into a police van. I was charged when I arrived at the police station and thrown into a cell, where I spent six hours alone. Eventually I was released, but I had the ordeal of having to tell my parents what had happened and the ordeal of going to a Juvenile Court at the age of 16.

Dad would often try and talk to me. If he couldn't reason with me with the Gospel, he would speak to me about my direction in life asking, "where do you think you will end up in life? You know, you can't live like this." Since I wasn't against God, or Jesus Christ, I would be open and quite willing to talk about these things. But clearly the pleasures of sin were greater, and I persisted in my sinful ways. Parties, friends, drinking became my world. Experimenting with drugs also had a hold on me, done purely to be part of the in-crowd. I was also followed by the police. On one occasion they followed me in the car, to right outside my house, breathalysed me and started to search me and the car. This incensed my parents, partly because a deacons' meeting was taking place at the house and as these men from church were leaving, there was the pastor's son at the end of the driveway being searched and breathalysed by the local constabulary! My father went out to challenge the Police. Afterwards, he warned me that I was living a dangerous life. I would ponder the things he said, not disbelieving them, yet not following through with them either.

In 1980, I was arrested by the police for a brawl at a club, along with nine others, some of whom were badly beaten up by the police. This happened on a Saturday night, which meant that my parents received a phone call from the police that I was in custody and would likely be there all day. You can imagine the worry that dad had when he went into the pulpit the next day. When I did get to come home, I surprisingly didn't receive a ticking off, but a sympathetic ear. I learned that this was because, before my release, several of my friends who were at the club and didn't get arrested, came around to see how I was. My mum invited them in, and they gave the story that it was all due to heavy handedness by the police. After several appearances at the Magistrates' Court, we were sent for trial at the Old Bailey. We were charged with "causing affray with intent to cause trouble." It was a long and complicated trial, which unknown to us, included an undercover policeman.Unknown to us, the police unit that was behind this undercover operation was the SPG (Special Patrol Group).

Already, the SPG had bad publicity at the time due to the killing of Blair Peach, an activist who was an anti-Nazi league supporter; it was rumoured, that he was killed by a blow to the head by one of six SPG officers. The actions of the SPG appalled my parents, and all the other boys' parents. Our lawyers were convinced we had a defence case, namely entrapment. This wasn't accepted by the judge, who said there was a case. This alarmed us all. During the trial I noticed that my parents were witnessing to all the boys and their parents. At the time I was embarrassed, but no-one else seemed to mind. After a lengthy trial, the jury dismissed eight out of the ten boys, which included me. Two were sent to a juvenile detention centre, but were later released. This did have repercussions. The police had been made to look foolish, and as a result I was followed around by the police, regularly being stopped and searched. Unfortunately for me, and a silly act on my part, I was later arrested and charged for carrying a knife.

At this point, I was getting tired of all of this, and a strong sense of dissatisfaction began to overwhelm me. The laughter, the fun, the wild nights experimenting with drugs and taking pills, having to duck and dive from every police car, was wearing thin. I somehow knew I had to escape from all of this, but I felt trapped. The question that my father asked me, "where are you going with all this?" was a question I often asked myself. But this sense of feeling trapped didn't last long.

God gave me an opportunity to turn to him. It

happened when the doorbell rang. My father answered the door. He came into the room where I was, looking furious with me. He said there were two police officers who wanted to speak to me for an alleged assault. As soon as I entered the hallway, the police asked if I was Timothy Wood? I said, I was. He then said he was arresting me for assault on a particular date and then cautioned me. He asked me to put my hands behind my back and handcuffed me. I looked up and saw my father's face, where there was a mixture of looks - despair, anger, worry. I asked him later what was going through his mind at the time? He said for a split second, he was angry with God, and angry with me, "but as soon as you went, your mother and I just got down to pray"; we were praying for you. As soon as we finished praying, I got on the phone with Roger (the solicitor who was a good friend of his), and he assured me that he would get on the phone with the police station.

When I arrived at the police station, the Custody Sergeant read out the charges. I protested my innocence. I knew that I wasn't involved in this fight, because I was elsewhere involved in another fight! Where I had been was no better, but I was not going to admit that. The usual routine happened: fingerprints, mug shots, shoelaces removed and into the cell, once again. Having been in police cells before, it is not something you wanted to get used to. I was lonely and afraid. All sorts of things were going on through my mind. I asked myself "is this where I am going to end up?" I now felt like the Prodigal Son in despair. But, I had a sudden awakening. What if I prayed? I still believe in God. What if I should talk to him? Would he answer? How could he answer? I really wanted to escape from the mess. This awakening was prompted by all the memories of how my parents taught us about God, and often they would say that people's lives are a mess because God is out of their lives. Is this why I was in a mess? I had no doubt that it was. I was in a crisis in my mind. Floods of memories filled my mind of the Bible stories I was taught. I remembered the story that my mother told about Jacob, how he wrestled with God all night. The story of the Prodigal Son came to mind.

I felt the best thing to do was to pray. I didn't care if the Custody Sergeant walked in, I was by now, determined to pray. So, I got down on my knees and started to pray. As I started to pray, I felt relieved. I didn't feel an overwhelming sense of worth, or any other emotional outburst, just relieved and the more I talked, the more relieved I was. I was relieved that after years of not praying, I could still pray. I was relieved that I believed he could hear me. In my prayers, I told him I knew this was all my doing and it was because of my sin that I was in this mess. I told him I believed in his son Jesus Christ, and I knew what needed to be done. I pleaded with him to take hold of my life and pleaded with him to forgive me. I even said a prayer to get me out of the cell within an hour. I couldn't believe it when the cell doors opened within that hour.

My solicitor and a policeman were standing at the door. For me, it was quite literally an experience of "I woke, the dungeon flamed with light, my chains fell off, my heart was free. I rose, went forth and followed thee."

The cell door opening within that hour: was that a coincidence or was it my answered prayer? I still don't know. But a sense of God's love began to take over. When I arrived home, I wasn't sure how to explain all that had happened to me in the cell to my parents. I wanted to, but in any case, they were more interested about the event. Did I assault the other man? No, I told them. Why then, did they arrest you? Did they treat you well?

I did try to explain to them that I did pray. Looking back on it, I think they thought this was me trying to sugarcoat things, and make them think that I was trying to seek their favour, but I wasn't. When I went to my room, I began pacing up and down, questioning my experience with God. I couldn't talk to them because they were filled with worry and annoyance at the police and me. But out of the corner of my eye, I saw a green Bible. I thought, maybe that's what I needed to do? Pick it up and read it. After all, my parents always said that the Bible is God's Word. So, I picked it up. It was very much a situation of "let's see where it leads me to." I opened it, and it was Mark's Gospel.

As I read it, I reminded myself of the fantastic life of Jesus Christ. It moved me. I flipped to Revelation, desperately hoping that God would speak to me. I came across chapter 3. 20 "Here I am. I stand at the door and knock." I now know this was an address written for the Church of Laodicea, but I didn't know that at the time and for me, it was an apt description of my sinful condition, that I had shut out Jesus Christ and he must come in. I then confessed all my sins. About a week later, I heard a series of talks on Jonah, how he had run away but the Lord backed him into a corner. Then I heard of how Jonah said in Chapter 2 verse 9, "salvation comes from the Lord." When I spoke to my dad, I'm not too sure if he believed me at first. I told my parents that I was not seeing my friends anymore, which hurt me, but I knew I had to make the break. It dawned on them that conversion had really and truly taken place. When I spoke to Dad later about my conversion and expressed sorrow and shame for making their lives difficult, he quoted Psalm 30 v.5, "weeping may remain for a night but rejoicing comes in the morning." His view was that it was worth it.

The outcome of the charges brought against me, was the day I arrived at Redbridge Magistrates Court and entered the dock. The Prosecution Counsel had the embarrassment of reporting to the Magistrate that none of the witnesses against me had turned up. The Magistrate gave the Counsel a ticking off, then turned to me and said I may go.

Although my father was thrilled to bits at my conversion, it pained him to see Christian parents having unconverted or wayward children, especially Pastors' children. I remember him writing to one Pastor, who had four children. Three of them were converted, the oldest wasn't. He later joined the Royal Marines. He didn't do anything to antagonise his parents, only that he just didn't want to know. His Pastor friend wrote back, simply thanking him for feeling his pain and burden.

Many parents came to him with this same burden, where children from Christian homes had become wayward or refused to speak to their parents. Some had not seen their children for years. Some lived lives of debauchery, drug-use, and ended up in prison. I tried to get my father to write or do a talk on parenting wayward children, but he never did. However, I do remember asking him once, "what would you say to a parent with wayward children?" Someone once told me of how he sought my father's help in this area. I asked him what my father had told him.

The first and foremost thing my father would tell any parent with wayward children is to remember Grace. That's not to say, just sit back and hope Grace intervenes. He would explain that parents had a responsibility to teach their children the Gospel, to train them in the way they should go and the way they should avoid. He would tell them that family prayers were crucial, Bible readings were important, and that children should be taken to church and instructed to go to church.

He would also argue that discipline was another important factor. I remember him once saying about a parent, "the trouble with so and so is that he never disciplined him" and would reference Eli and Eli's sons. Eli's failure was that he never corrected his sons, and in this way, James never ignored parents' responsibilities to their children. Indeed, at dedications, he would always emphasise this and tell parents of their responsibility, to train children in the ways of the Gospel. Yet although he emphasised parents' responsibilities, he always said that as much as a parent may fulfil their duty, and do so honourably, it doesn't achieve salvation or merit salvation. That's why he argued that a faithful parent fulfilling their duty was just as dependent on the Grace of God as a parent who was reckless. I remember him once saying "as much as he owed everything to the prayers of his mother, it wasn't her prayers that saved him, but Grace." That's why he would tell those with wayward children to seek God's Grace further.

Secondly, he would tell them that persevering prayer is important. He would remind those with wayward children that it would be a testing process for them, and the Lord does test parents to see how much trust they have in God. I remember my mother telling me how they used to have seasons of prayers for my conversion, which would include fasting. I once heard James say to someone, don't ever give up committing your children to the hands of God. For him, it wasn't just that, but it was comforting for him, knowing that he could commit his children to "the hands of God."

Thirdly, he would remind them to set an example of faith in Jesus Christ and commitment to the Gospel. There was a time in my life, where I was hostile to the Gospel, that any mention of Christ, God, or coming to church, would have been met with slammed doors. My parents never forced the Gospel down my throat. They knew that this, perhaps, would antagonise me. Yet, they never slammed the doors on me or shut me out, but treated me normally with love, patience, and kindness. I remember him talking to a Christian parent, who had a son who never spoke to his parents. He would go upstairs, straight from work. He would come down for dinner, never spoke, and as soon as dinner was finished, he would go out. Dad spoke to them at length, by reminding them that they were doing everything right, and all they could do was show Christian love by example.

Fourthly, he would remind parents to be a friend to their children. Know their interests and then show an interest in their interests. Speak to them as a friend. Don't challenge them too much, just be by their side.

Last of all, Dad would always remind those with wayward children of the sovereignty of God, which means having to wait on God's own time for him to be gracious. If our sons and daughters are chosen by God and redeemed by Jesus Christ, they will be born again by the Holy Spirit at God's appointed time. To be reminded of the sovereignty of God, is to believe that all things are in his hands, including wayward children. It's to believe that God may use extraordinary circumstances in different situations, and that God will intervene when the time is right for him to do so.

For these reasons, James would use my testimony to encourage those with wayward children to never give up hope, because his own prodigal son returned.

# 11

## MISSIONARY ENDEAVOURS

JAMES WAS VERY MISSIONARY-MINDED. HE SUPPORTED missions both home and abroad. In fact, he told me that he wanted to be a missionary. This was something he shared with Ailsa, who was also open to the idea. Ailsa had an aunt who was a missionary in India for over 50 years, working with BMMF. India, for them, became a real possibility. James told me that he was disappointed in many churches' lack of vision for missions. When he was younger, his church and many others had so many missionaries who they would send out and support missionaries. This is why James' Broadmead years focused so much on missions. He believed that his ministry, during those years, should be encouraging mission work as much as possible, by opening people's minds to the possibility of being called into the ministry. Many were.

I remember as a child being told many stories of missionaries: Hudson Taylor, William Carey, CT Studd and Eric Liddell, as well as stories of missionaries whose works were not recorded. My parents loved to tell these stories. This probably explains why James loved to travel. For a man who grew up in the 1930s and 40s, James had done a fair amount of travelling, mainly because of his Army years. His army career had taken him throughout most of Northern Europe. An opportunity for further travel arose for him in 1963, when James alongside another Pastor called Clive Tyler, who was nearby in Alsager, were asked to lead a group of students from the London Bible College to travel by bus to Israel.

Clive had also been trained at LBC and later went to South Africa to become Principal of the Bible Institute in Cape Town. They purchased a retired single decker bus from Manchester Corporation and refitted it to take the necessary water, fuel, and food stores, as well as tents and other necessities. Ernest Kevan believed it was important for these students to see the key places in the history of Christianity, but mainly to see the sights in Israel. It cost £60 per student for a 7-week trip. This trip was recorded in the Crewe Chronicle because it caused a bit of a stir, and potentially could have caused diplomatic problems. It took place during the cold war period, which meant passing through parts of the Iron Curtain and Middle Eastern countries, who did not look favourably upon anyone going to Israel. There was also another reason for the trip. It was to try and meet up with Christians in these parts, along the way, to encourage them and distribute Christ-centred literature and Bibles. This meant having to smuggle and hide these works, to the best of their abilities. Iron Curtain and Muslim countries would not only confiscate these types of literature, but they would also put you in prison, as they made it very clear that all Bibles were forbidden.

They started their 7,000-mile-long trip, driving through Belgium, Germany, and Austria. It was upon leaving Austria that their troubles started. At all border checks they were ordered to get out of the bus and line up, while their bus was thoroughly checked. This meant waiting for many hours, and it was tense, with guards at times pointing their rifles at the passengers. It was no laughing matter. However, on the border of Bulgaria, something did happen that helped release the tension.

Everyone was lined up in a straight line. The guards were doing their standard, thorough, search of the bus and were quite close to where the Bibles were hidden; something happened that distracted the guards by making them laugh, although the party believed it to be providential. One of the students had a bit of a dodgy tummy, and insisted that he should have a toilet roll with him. Situated on a slight slope, this student dropped the roll accidentally, and the end got caught in his pocket, while the toilet paper rolled down and unravelled itself in between the travellers and the guards. Everyone started to stare at it with amusement, and some light snickering started, which developed into roars of laughter from both the travellers and the guards. This lightened the atmosphere, and the guards let them pass through without any more searching, meaning that the concealed Bibles were not discovered!

Entering Turkey was a challenge. The journey was long and hot, yet the giving out of literature was still happening in the towns and villages when opportunities presented themselves. This was received with a mixture of suspicion and cautious gratitude. James was one of the three drivers, and he said in the Crewe Chronicle that the roads were shocking and often, "we had to get out and push the bus up steep hills."

One sense of tension remains to some amusement. James was being given gratuitous advice on how to drive by one of the students, and having had enough he cynically snapped back, "now listen sonny, I was driving tanks ten times the size of this bus when you were running about in your short pants." It was something about the delivery and the way he said it that just made the travellers roar with laughter, and the way Dad told the story became one of our favourite memories of him.

They were able to reach the Hagia Sophia and then managed to get into Istanbul. They then met up with a Pastor, who spent much time piecing together old Bibles. They were also able to give out tracts and literature. Overall, people were quite receptive. However, when they passed through Galatia through the Cilician Gates just by the Syrian border, after a four-day journey, trouble was awaiting them.

Apparently while in Istanbul, a group of Christians had been unwisely causing trouble. They were not thought to be genuine, but agitators. The police were waiting for them by the Turkey-Syrian border. They were ordered out of the bus and had it thoroughly searched. James was one of the six that was taken into custody and had his passport confiscated. Altogether, they were held in custody for three days. The police had accused them of distributing Bibles and Christian books in villages. A

British Consul was called, who complained on their behalf that this would only further damage relations between the two countries, threatening them with making it onto the news. I remember Dad telling me that the conditions were not pleasant at all. A local town official became involved and settled their differences, and the group was granted permission to continue. In the Crewe Chronicle, James explained, "we got a little worried here."

Having been allowed to pass through into Syria, they were watched like hawks. As they journeyed through Syria, the people were not at all receptive. They treated these Western tourists with disgust. One student took a picture of a group of youths who then turned on him, and started throwing rocks and stones at the bus, smashing a window, all while James was driving. As a result, they couldn't make much contact with people. Syria back then, as it remains today, was a very dangerous country.

To make up for lost time, the party travelled through the night. On one occasion, they were forced by the army to stop and camp in the dark. When they woke up the next morning they found themselves beneath skull and crossbow warning signs, and they realised that they were on a firing range!

They arrived at Damascus, a city of expectation, but a city with which they were ultimately disappointed. This was due to the civil unrest, barricaded public buildings, tanks in the streets, soldiers everywhere, and civilians running around with machine guns. They arrived in Jordan and then crossed the Allenby Bridge into Israel, where they spent the next week travelling around the land of Abraham, Moses, the Prophets, the Apostles, and the early Christian Church. During that time, this was a big adventure for them. Today perhaps, not so much, as it would be easy to catch an aeroplane. But back then, that was not the case. One thing that struck all the students about James, was that despite travelling in the heat and dust, James always stayed perfectly smart. He somehow managed to have iron pressed trousers. It's hardly surprising that one of the students who eventually became a pastor, said that James was the best dressed minister in the Christian world.

A week was spent in Jerusalem, and then a few days around the Holy Land. They then returned by ship from Haifa to Naples, with the bus on board. Subsequently, they drove overland through Italy, Pompeii, Florence, Rome and onward via France back to Crewe. Their only transport problem was four punctures and a broken wheel spring. Travelling through those many countries and cultures, not only opened their eyes to the benefits that Britain owed to the gospel, but also to the need for foreign missionary endeavours, which became so important in James' future ministry. To go through parts of the world, where the word of God was forbidden, bothered James. That's why he was such a strong supporter of Open Doors and other Christian organisations that supported Christians behind the Iron Curtain. I remember well, the stories told by the pastors who were thrown out of countries or those who were allowed to come to Britain and came to stay with us.

When James moved to London, as already noted, he

had more missionary opportunities. He not only became a board member of Regions Beyond Missionary Union (RBMU) but was also a member of the personnel committee and was given the role of Pastoral brief for the missionaries. Janet Helens, who was sent out to Peru and was a member at Broadmead, gave James this opportunity. James had a real concern for South America, but it was Africa that became James' love. While still pastor in Broadmead, he was asked to go to Africa, Zaire, and Kenya. While in Zaire, he spent time with RBMU missionaries Robert and Dorothy Dear. He then travelled to Kenya, where he met up with Keith and Priscilla Underhill. He also met up with John Langat, with whom Jonathan had stayed previously. He then met up with Lawrence Bomett, who later started an organisation called "Africans Reaching Africa" which aimed to equip local people to reach their own indigenous people.

It was arranged that James should go from village to village while in Kenya. This involved travelling through the heart of Kenya, through the jungle and the mud. When he arrived at villages, he was greeted by all the villagers who would come out of their homes, intrigued not so much by a Westerner preaching the gospel, but by a man with white hair. He remembers on one occasion, leaving one village, when something caught his eye; he saw a man sprinting through the woods, through the jungle and then he disappeared. When he arrived at the next village, he found that the villagers were out of their homes ready to greet him. This man had run from his village to the next, to tell them that a man from the West is coming and that, "he's got white hair." As James and

Ailsa reached this village, they were overwhelmed by the welcome they received. James then, from the truck, stood up, opened the Bible, and preached to them for around 45 minutes.

In 1982 James went to South Africa, having been invited to speak at the Bible institute in Cape Town. He gave a "memorable series of lectures on the Song of Solomon." He preached several times in the Cape Town Baptist Church while there. The church there wanted to call him to be their pastor, but there was a charismatic issue which prevented him from going. As already mentioned, he spent 18 months in Africa in the mid-80s. I don't think James returned to Africa after that, apart from a much shorter visit to South Africa in the late 90s, but his love for Africa and his burden to pray for Africa, never faded.

James was concerned about the home front as much as abroad. He was a strong supporter of the railway mission, SASRA, the Crewe railway mission, and the Liverpool Mission, but he had a real concern for London. He met with, and knew many pastors from North East London, especially in areas where pastors were not so well supported. He was particularly supportive of the London City Mission, and he encouraged people from Broadmead to consider spending their summer periods helping the London City Mission. One of the young men who took on this role was Timothy Hull, who eventually felt called to work full time for the London City Mission. Having his good friend Chris Frohwein, an elder at Broadmead, provided James with many opportunities to support the work of the London City Mission. James'

burden for London was seen by Michael Toogood, a
Grace Baptist Minister who felt called to go and work in
the heart of Soho and plant a church there. In many
ways, James and Michael were alike, in their immaculate,
smart, dress code. Michael Toogood asked James to be on
the board of what became known as "The London In-
Reach Project." This included the work at Covent
Garden. This was a challenge that James rose to, eventually becoming its chairman.

James' missionary heart remained with him until his
dying days. Even though he had returned to the UK, he
remained in touch with, supported, and encouraged the
missionaries with whom he had worked, so much so, that
my brothers and I received many emails from former
pastors and missionaries after he died, saying that he was
so helpful and key in their encouragement.

James retired from the role of Pastor in 1998, at the age
of 67, after 42 years of service. Walthamstow Baptist
Church was filled with many of James' friends and
former members, who came to express their gratitude for
his ministry and to wish him a happy retirement. Tributes were read from different parts of the world: Kenya,
Zaire, South Africa, Australia, America, and Canada.
Although he had retired from the pastorate, he never
fully retired. He continued to be the chairman of the
London In-Reach Project, supporting missionaries and
encouraging young men into the ministry. He kept in
touch with all his friends via regular correspondence, but
he phoned closer friends on a very regular basis, and
would visit or go on holidays with some of them.

Nothing gave him greater pleasure than to return to

his Lancashire roots, especially visiting his brother Peter, who lived on a 500-acre farm, near Clitheroe. There he would meet up with his old school friends, and as president of the Old Boltonians, he would enjoy school reunions. By now, his family was growing, with his sons married and the arrival of grandchildren. Again, this gave him so much pleasure. James and Ailsa had always prayed for their sons and that, of course, included any young ladies to whom they would one day be married. As soon as James arrived in Crewe in 1956, there was an advert for his induction in the Crewe Chronicle. A few miles away in Sandbach, a couple were themselves looking for a church to attend. Having seen the advert (and believing that anyone who had trained under Ernest Kevan must be sound!), Clarence and Barbara Jefferies, along with their young son Tim, started to attend West Street Baptist Church and became firm and life-long friends. They had two further children, both daughters, one of whom was called Sara. Who knew that, one day, Sara would walk down the aisle with Jonathan and provide four grandchildren: Abigail, James, Samuel and Esther. James rejoiced to have met one great-grandchild, Ava, before his death.

After his time at the London Theological Seminary, Tim served alongside Robert Winston at Belhus Park Chapel in South Ockendon, Essex. Amongst all the things of benefit that Tim took from Robert was his daughter, Susan! Tim and Susan gave James and Ailsa the joy of a further four grandchildren: Thomas, Bethany, Jonathan and David. They were both very proud of their daughters in law, Sara and Susan. Ailsa, along with James was able to see Abigail marry in 2014 before entering glory exactly four weeks later. James was also able to see the marriages of Thomas to Rachael, Bethany to Nathan and James to Katie.

Yet, as he looked back at his ministry, he said he had many regrets. There were certain things that he wished he had done differently, and that there were certain roads he wished he hadn't gone down. This surely is a thing with which many retired pastors battle.

One of his biggest regrets was not seeing the work of the spirit in revival. Revival to James, was the church's last hope. For James, the church was not in a healthy state, and he often expressed great disappointment in the direction the church was headed. That's why, as much as possible, he encouraged people to get a grasp of what revival is, and why it was so desperately needed. He encouraged people in his churches to read revival accounts as much as possible. He encouraged people to read Lloyd-Jones' sermons on revival, saying that this was Dr Lloyd Jones at his very best. He encouraged people to read other works on revival like, "Time of Refreshing" and "Second Evangelical Awakening" by Edwin Orr, Brian Edward's book on revival, and many more. He believed that people needed to be reminded and refreshed of its need. I mention this because of James' role in the Reformation and Revival Fellowship Movement.

Originally called the "Baptist Revival Fellowship", BRF was a yearly conference held in November, with an accompanying bulletin twice a year, and a membership of about 1,400 people. It had a committee, who would meet for prayer and decide on the speakers for the annual conference. There were other denominational fellowships for revival, like the Methodists, Congregationalists, and Anglicans, but the BRF was the strongest and the only one that endured. It started in the 1930s when a group of Baptist ministers met for prayer, longing for revival. Reverend Theo Bamber of Rye Lane Baptist Church in Peckham was the prime motivator behind this. Other ministers, such as Geoff King of the East London Tabernacle, Angus Macmillan, Ernest Rudman, Leslie Lyall, and Hugh Butt met together to pray. This continued to grow as other leaders joined. As a result, the Baptist Revival Fellowship came about. It was felt that a residential conference would be the best way to continue. So as of 1954, a yearly conference on revival, with a Bible study, and meeting for prayer was held at High Leigh in Hertfordshire. This proved to be so popular, they had to limit the number. In the 1960s there were 350 people present at the conference and it moved to Swanwick in Derbyshire. James didn't attend the first two conferences, but he attended in 1956 and then made it his annual conference trip. He loved conferences, and would go to a few, but the "Banner of Truth" and the "Revival Fellowship" conferences were his favourites.

Dr Martyn Lloyd-Jones was a regular speaker in the early days, as was Ernest Kevan, Leith Samuel, and David Pawson, among others. But just as there were changes in the evangelical scene, so too were there changes at the conference. Since the attendees were largely Baptist Union men, a situation arose that the BRF couldn't ignore.

In 1971, the Principal of the Manchester Baptist College, Michael Taylor, caused a stir, which prompted inevitable divisions. At the annual assembly of the Baptist Union, held at Westminster Chapel, he spoke on the subject, "how much of a man is Jesus Christ?" In his statement, he not only questioned the deity of Christ, but he actually denied it. He said, "it could not be claimed that he was the Son of God. We must stop short of saying unequivocally that this is God." This clearly, is a contradiction to the claims of Christ. This caused a stir in the Baptist Union, and as a result, many churches left, while others opted to remain. This affected the BRF. Those who had left the Baptist Union felt that the association with the B.U. was problematic because of the controversy, while others believed that distancing themselves from the Baptist Union wasn't necessary. Additionally, there were individuals who were caught in the middle, possibly attending BRF gatherings or events but finding it difficult to completely separate from the Baptist Union. BRF was not officially associated with the Baptist Union, which allowed them to take a clear position on the matter and communicate their stance to the Baptist Union. The Baptist Union didn't agree with Michael Taylor's perspective but also didn't take any decisive action regarding the situation. Consequently, BRF faced the 1970s with smaller numbers, but was still well attended. It became an unusual atmosphere. Fresh and new faces joined, James was invited onto the committee, and the fellowship started again, still longing and praying for revival. But another storm was brewing.

Towards the second half of the 70s and into the early

80s, there were many churches who adopted the trends of the charismatic movement. There were some who came to BRF who had been drawn towards them and wanted to incorporate its approach into the annual conference. This created a different atmosphere. Some tried to hijack the meetings with over emphasis on music, while some attempted to speak in tongues during times of prayer. Then there were groupings and hand-picked prayer meetings. The committee meetings were less united, because there were some who were advocating these convictions, causing a great deal of tension. Numbers were now beginning to fall, but James felt like he should stay on. He and others felt that the reformed emphasis on the centrality of the preached word of God and prayer, was the only way forward. They did not believe that these were conditions for revival, believing that revival would only happen by God's sovereign and gracious act. However, they believed that this was the only way forward. As a result of their stance, there was a very unpleasant conference, where David Pawson announced that he had visited a railway museum on his way to Swanwick, and saw all the old trams and steam engines, which reminded him of the present conference, "all machinery and no life." That night, he packed his bags and left.

Those who also favoured the charismatic trend, by and large, did not return, choosing to go elsewhere for their meetings. Those who stayed behind were saddened, not only because of the split, but also because a lot of good people of the reformed persuasion also left. The committee felt there ought to be a new direction. Originally, the chairman held the post for three years before another member of the committee became its chairman. When James became chairman, he thought it was going to be for three years, but the committee felt strongly that James should continue as chairman, and as such he remained so. Little did he know, he would remain chairman for 23 years. When he expressed his unease about being chairman for this long, they assured him that he was the best man for the job. Many felt a change of name and disassociating themselves from the past was the way forward. By now, the Methodist revival fellowship drifted and disappeared, as did that of the Congregationalist church. A new name was suggested and tried, "Fellowship for Revival." After a couple of years, the suggestion to be changed to the "Reformation and Revival Fellowship," which emphasised and held onto its reformed position, was agreed upon.

After 23 years, James made it clear that he was becoming old and tired, and that although he would continue to attend and support the fellowship, he could not continue as chairman. The committee and conference were saddened by this but thanked him unanimously for all his hard work and effort. But why did he remain loyal to the fellowship? After all those years of upset, wouldn't it have been better if he had moved on elsewhere, or not go altogether?

Firstly, on the charismatic issue, he felt that those who favoured it, had missed the point, and lost its vision. James never favoured charismatic emphases and he had his reasons, both theological and practical. He felt that charismatic emphasis was shallow and superficial.

However, he had friends who had charismatic tendencies. As much as he wouldn't agree with them, he would put it to one side and would continue to regard them as brothers and sisters in Christ, if they genuinely held onto the view of new birth. However, he didn't feel that the charismatics of the BRF were prepared to do that. He felt that the charismatics were not focussing on prayer and the study of God's word at the BRF, its main goal. Their emphasis was more about the gifts and worship, and he couldn't go along with this.

Secondly, James was concerned with the formality of the reformed position. As much as he held onto the reformed principles and loved reading reformed material, he had a fear of formality in the reformed position. Sometimes, he could understand why people thought the reformed position was dull. Lloyd-Jones had a concern about this as well. James was concerned about subjective experiences. Indeed, he had seen this harm many good Christians, but he also had concern about excluding feeling altogether. That's why he loved BRF, because he felt the conference was open to this.

Thirdly, he just loved the conference. Not even the cold air of November would put him off. James continued going to the conference, until he was 86. Towards the end of his days he could feel the cold more and more. Yet, this didn't put him off from attending. He loved the warmth of the fellowship, renewing friendships year after year, and meeting old and new friends.

But the most important thing of all, was the desperate need of the hour. James prayed every day for revival, yet the conference gave to him a buzz and a greater longing for it to happen. And with a shared vision and a shared longing, he knew that the conference attendees had the same yearning. There is no need to present our case for this great need for revival and reformation; the sleaze, the corruption, the immorality, and the decline of the Christian Church cries out for it. The need for the warmth of fellowship, powerful preaching, a longing for the power and presence of the Holy Spirit to fall on the church, is the crying need of the hour.

James never had the privilege of seeing revival, as indeed many Christians haven't, but I know that his dying prayer was for God to restore the honour of his name, for the church to come alive, to cherish and hunger after God's word, and for souls to be saved. As God has done it before, can he not do it again?

And if we should ever, by God's grace, experience revival, then it's due to the prayers of God's people including people like James Wood, that we can thank.

# 12

# FINAL YEARS

AFTER TAKING ON RETIREMENT, JAMES REMAINED BUSY. Keeping up with friends and his extended family was important to him and he loved to hear news of his nieces and nephews, as well as his brothers and sisters in law. He spent a lot of time writing letters of encouragement, and even managed to master email with a little help from his daughter-in-law, Susan, and later much technical support from his youngest grandson, David. Since he was now free on Sundays, he did a lot of itinerant preaching, especially around the London area. He felt the strain of doing a lot of travelling and tried to do as little as possible. When he retired, he returned to some of his hobbies: flying his model aeroplanes, oil painting, going to railway exhibitions, meeting up with old friends as much as possible, and even going on holidays with good friends. James and Ailsa travelled with Keith and Marje Mawdsley to Boston, took a cruise to Norway, and visited Switzerland and Italy with Nigel and Helen Cooke. Ailsa and James continued all their missionary commitments, but bit by bit, they began to step away from them. They felt that fresh faces and new blood, younger people, should take over. For those that did take over, they always offered their support and advice. When James stepped down from his position as Pastor at Walthamstow Central Baptist Church, he supported the church in almost immediately calling Roger Neil to be the pastor, who served the church until his own retirement. Meanwhile James and Ailsa looked for a new place to live, outside of London; they wanted to embrace a slower life.

There was talk of them returning North, back to their roots of Lancashire, possibly Cumbria. They would have loved to return there. The one thing that kept them from doing so was the family. Like all proud parents and grandparents, they thought the world of their family. By 2002, they had all their grandchildren, 8 of them. But more than that, they rejoiced in seeing that all three of their sons and their 8 grandchildren were saved. James had the joy of seeing all his grandchildren baptised. Ailsa saw 6 of them. There was never a moment when they thought that they played a part in this, and they stressed it was all by the grace of God. Ailsa, in particular, thumped this point into the preachers of the family saying, "don't forget to talk about grace," or "Did you refer to the grace of God?"

To stay relatively near their family, they decided to move to the Essex Coast in Thorpe, near Frinton. Having had friends from the days of Broadmead nearby, this helped them settle down quickly. They had a beach hut on the coast at Frinton, which was an added excitement for the grandchildren, when they visited their grandparents. Having a dog gave them the motivation for exercise, and James loved taking Chloe the labrador along the coast and the countryside. They were always hospitable, and loved to entertain as much as possible, and friends from afar would come to stay with them: missionaries, former pastors, college friends and more. But those that gave them the greatest joy, were former members of their churches. Hearing someone had gone into full-time Christian work would also bring them great joy. Anyone who came to stay was treated like they were in a 5-star hotel. It got to the point where they were so busy, the boys and their families would have to arrange times to meet and see them.

Bank holiday weekends were always free, so that the families could come together. The excitement, for the children, was staying overnight and then heading off to the beach, coming back to Ailsa's famous food. After a while, James would sneak back into his study, because he could never cope with all the noise, whereas Ailsa thrived on it.

As time went by, James did less and less preaching and travelling, which meant having to find a church to settle in. They eventually chose Fordham, on the outskirts of Colchester, a Church of England with evangelical persuasion. The church welcomed them as loved members of the family. For James, it fascinated him that it used to be the parish of one of his favourite puritans, John Owen. It is rumoured that it was while John Owen was vicar of Fordham that he wrote his most famous book, "Death of Death."

There was some reluctance on the part of James and

Ailsa to return to their Church of England roots, but they felt that Fordham was staunchly evangelical, and they decided to stay. They were not the sort of people to just sit back and they got involved. For some years, James led a "growth group," as well as home groups. He also did book reviews, and on occasion preached. Ailsa got involved in the work of the church with the women. People from Fordham have written to say that they were like the spiritual parents, calling at times for their wisdom, encouragement, and prayers. For the years that they were there, they were very happy.

But their lives were not plain sailing. Ailsa suffered from arthritis for years, especially in her back and neck. As James grew older, he suffered from asthma more and more, eventually developing COPD, along with the deterioration of his hearing. The ministry has a price and having two sons in the ministry as well, was an added burden for them. The end of Jonathan's ministry at Whittlesey was not a happy one, and resulted in him having to leave the church, which caused heartbreak for the whole family. It pained James and Ailsa to watch this happen and to listen to the pain their grandchildren were suffering. Sadly, Marcus' marriage had broken down, and they divorced. These are the pains of any parents. Nevertheless, they remained faithful and were constantly rejoicing that their children and grandchildren's names are in the Lamb's Book of Life.

2014 became a life changer for James. In February, Ailsa was diagnosed with Leukaemia. Despite knowing the slim chances of recovery, Ailsa did not once become overtly negative about the situation and remained very spiritual. She suffered with constant nose bleeds, which made her stay up all night. The exhaustion of constantly trying to look after her took its toll on James too.

Her deterioration was rapid, but there was one thing she pleaded to the Lord for, and that was that she would be able to attend the wedding of her first granddaughter, Abigail. The whole family knew this was going to be difficult, but with the help of her sister-in-law Victoria, and brother-in-law Peter, including other members of the family, she was able to enjoy the day, seeing her son, not only give away his daughter, but also conducting the service. As much as she enjoyed the day, it took a lot out of her. The time had come when she felt it was right to go into a hospice. From the day she arrived, she made it clear that she was a Christian and she was not afraid of dying. Many relatives and friends came to see Ailsa during that period, and they all testified that she was full of hope, ready for glory.

Four days before she passed away, I went to see her, and saw how tired my dad was. I told him to go and get some rest, and that I would stay with mum. I read to her Isaiah 6 and 7, and then we talked a little.

All of a sudden, I said, "Mum, why are you smiling?" She simply responded, "because I've got glory waiting ahead of me, I've got all these eternal treasures right before me, the only snag is leaving you behind."

After this, Dad was constantly by her side, reading the scriptures to her and praying. As she got weaker, and the medication increased, she began drifting into a state of unconsciousness.

A strange thing happened before she passed away.

James was sitting in the armchair, falling asleep, when Ailsa sat up and started conducting. There was no music being played anywhere, and James asked her if she was alright. She may have been conducting the angels that serenaded her into heaven. Half an hour later, she passed away and reached the sandy shores of Jordan. Jonathan and Marcus were also present for her passing.

The day after was difficult for James because it was his birthday. We gathered as a family to be with him and tried to make it an enjoyable day for him, whilst grieving a wonderful wife, mother, and grandmother.

This began a new direction for James. The first year was tough, but he had many friends who kept in touch with him, and that kept him going. One such friend was Reg Fidler, who had been the treasurer and deacon at Broadmead, and was now living in Frinton quite close to James. As two elderly widowers they enjoyed meeting up once a week for a cup of tea and a chat. Reg had a remarkable testimony. During World War 2 he was the pilot of a Wellington Bomber. His good friend had been killed on one mission and Reg went to visit his widow to console her. Over time they developed a friendship and he asked to marry her. She refused him because he was not a Christian and started to tell him the gospel. Some while later he was flying on a mission to Germany and was shot down. As he was coming down, he realised he was not a Christian and cried out to the Lord to save him. After crash landing in Germany, he managed to escape to Switzerland where the Swiss authorities arrested him. He escaped back into Germany and made his way to Spain and Gibraltar. On his return to Britain, he visited his friend's wife again and explained what had happened. This time she accepted his proposal, and they were married. Reg passed away a year before James and James was privileged to conduct his funeral service.

There was a change of church for James also. He had stopped attending Fordham as regularly, due to the distance from his home, and started to attend Kirby-Le-Soken Evangelical Church. It was a small and elderly church, and because it was nearer to him, James decided it should be the church he attended. Some former members of Broadmead were already members there, such as Chris and Johanna Frohwein and Maralyn Lamont. A new man had taken up the pastorate there, Ken Houghton. James often commented on the fact that Ken was a real pastor, and a pastor to him, saying that all his years of being a pastor meant he never had a pastor for himself. James did continue to preach at various churches, but as time went by he reduced his preaching engagements and latterly he would only preach once on a Sunday. The last time he preached away from his home church was at my church in Wigmore, Kent on 4th October 2015.

The 28th July 2016 was the last time he preached at Kirby, and after that he declined any offers. He did take some Bible studies at Kirby, and his last one was on the 13th of November in 2019, when his theme was, "wait." In his studies, he made it clear that God calls us to be active, but there are moments when he tells us to wait. This was a very apt theme for a man, who made it known to select friends, that he was tired and ready to go to glory. He never mentioned this to his family because he was a positive man.

There are a number of things to point out during this period. James gave himself over to prayer, he was always a prayer warrior. He never hesitated in leading family prayers, concluding every event with friends in prayer, praying in the place of worship. Wherever he went, he was a man who was devoted to prayer. He would spend many hours in prayer. He continued to pray for revival. He prayed for God to vindicate himself more and more. He had a real burden for souls and prayed for more conversions. He prayed for pastors and missionaries, he prayed for friends and neighbours, but most of all, his family. In this sense, he seemed to find prayer natural. He had a telephone ministry where he would phone people up on a regular basis, to enquire after their health, both physically and spiritually. Being a pastor's pastor, he would regularly phone younger men in the ministry.

I noticed an added note to his prayers. He was always rejoicing. I remember phoning him once, and I asked how he was getting on, "I'm just rejoicing," was his response; he was always positive, even when his health began to deteriorate. There were at least two occasions where we thought it was the end, and somehow he bounced back. His movement was limited, and he needed walking sticks, then a frame, and later a wheelchair. In all that time, he never once complained to anyone else about himself, he only ever had time for other people. Never once did he make a fuss about his illness, he just got on with it. He once said, "I am like an old car, once one part of the car goes wrong, you fix it, and then something else goes wrong."

On Boxing Day, 2018, whilst staying in Peterborough, he was taken into hospital by ambulance in tremendous pain. We all visited, thinking this might be the end for him. However, despite spending three weeks in the City Hospital, Peterborough, and then two more weeks in Colchester and Harwich, he rallied at the start of 2019. Before long, to the amazement of us all, he was soon back at home, albeit with extra help being provided.

James had more and more trips to hospitals in his last years, as well as respite in care homes, but this was not the way he wanted to live. He wanted independence in his own home. This began to be a problem for the family. While his fighting spirit wouldn't stop, the increasing worry of him having a fall or collapsing with no one around to help him was taking its toll. The tough decision facing the family, but mainly Jonathan, Marcus, and I, was soon taken out of our hands. He developed a UTI, which meant a return to the hospital at the end of February 2020. This was to be his final hospital stay.

By Thursday 5th March, he had entered a state of semi-consciousness. On the Friday, all three of us sons along with Sara and Susan were able to see him and spend some time with him. Some other members of the family gathered around his bed across that weekend. The threat of the Coronavirus was hovering, but we still praise God that he was able to meet his Maker before the virus forced the country into lockdown. This meant that for James' last few days, he was still able to have someone with him. The nurses and care he had was second to

none. They said that they had come across many "fight-
ers" in their time, but they were so shocked and in awe of
how long it was taking for James to let go. In fact, I heard
one nurse, while stroking his hair, say, "come on now
James, your sons have told you, glory is awaiting your
arrival."

The nurses did not hesitate to reassure us at how
peaceful he looked, and how content he was. As a family
we couldn't really tell, but these medical professionals
could, saying there were no signs of stress, and that he
was just peaceful and content.

His long fight at the end, meant that the family didn't
know how long they should stay. Marcus was present
most of the time, but it was more of a struggle for me and
particularly Jonathan, as we lived further away. So, we
stayed in Dad's house, until, on Wednesday 11th of March
2020, at around 11AM, Marcus phoned to say, "Dad has
passed to glory."

Jonathan and I breathed a sigh of relief and then
immediately responded with prayer, praising God for the
life of our Dad and what he personally meant to us as a
family but mainly as a father, praising God that he had
finished the fight and gone to be with his Saviour, or to
use a phrase he often used, "to see the Lamb on the
throne."

The funeral service was set for the 27th of March at All
Saints Fordham, so that James could be buried with his
beloved wife Ailsa. We were so overwhelmed with the
messages of comfort and condolences. Despite many
people wanting to come and pay their respects at the

funeral, the restrictions of Coronavirus prohibited them from being able to do so.

With the country in lockdown, the number allowed to attend a funeral was severely restricted. The rules meant that family members only were allowed to attend; this had to be out of doors and adhering to social distancing protocols. The service, therefore, was very small, held at the graveside. Even the vicar who was due to lead the service had to cancel at the last minute, due to self-isolation. It was a beautiful crisp sunny day in early spring. The grounds were peaceful, and the immediate family was there: James' sons, daughters-in-law, grandchildren and their spouses, and, at our insistence, Maralyn Lamont too, a faithful friend to James.

The assistant vicar led, and James' pastor, Pastor Ken, spoke beautifully to the family from 2 Timothy Chapter 4. Then Jonathan spoke deeply from the heart in his eulogy for Dad, and everyone there was encouraged by his strong words. We were then able to sing two hymns, with no accompaniment, "I Stand Amazed in the Presence" and, "Thine be the Glory." Even the undertakers were surprised at how well we sang!

Even though the service was not the fitting tribute the family had in mind, they took comfort in the fact that regardless of how small or how large the service was, it wouldn't affect James' position in glory. As James' brother-in-law Robin said, "James was humble enough for that to happen."

# AFTERWORD

The attempt to write the story of James' life was entirely as a result of the Coronavirus. If the service were to have gone ahead as planned, then there would have been fitting tributes. I want to assure you, that although Dad had an interesting life, there was no attempt on my part to magnify his life, or compare him to someone great, but rather just to pay tribute to someone who did make a difference in so many people's lives. That difference wasn't a temporary occurrence, the difference has eternal value. Dad described his life, and his ministry as very ordinary. Really, being ordinary means keeping humble, and not doing things to be noticed; Dad never sought that. What was in his heart the whole time, were the churches that he served. He wasn't looking for big numbers or fame, he was looking at the health and the spiritual welfare of God's people. Sometimes you can see the effect of that. There are famous names who you hear about, conference speakers and writers, but some of those very people have churches with little impact. It makes you wonder, have they neglected their responsibility of pastoring the flock? Dad never neglected his flock. In fact, Dad loved his flock with an aching love. Even those who were plotting against him, he loved them fully enough to give them the benefit of the doubt. But of course, this didn't always work out.

The problem with what Dad called ordinary, was that this had an impact on himself. When he was deep into his retirement, he had certain regrets. That's how the great enemy of God works. He puts things into our heads. But by his own admission, God was gracious to him, and reminded him that it's about being faithful, and Dad was exactly that. He remained faithful to the very end by God's grace. But God gave Dad a blessing once, a reminder, that no matter how one may feel in our failures, He continues to do good and work His purposes and plans. This happened once when I had a phone call from him. There was something different about the tone of his voice. Normally, he would ask first about how I was, and how the family was. But on this occasion he didn't. He said, "Tim, I'm just rejoicing."

"Why?" I asked.

"Well, I just had a phone call and I had to tell someone. A man called me and said, 'are you James Wood the ex-Minister at Crewe? Well, you won't know me, but I know you. You see, I had a brother who was 8 at the time, and he became very sick and was dying. You asked my parents if you could see him every week and tell him bible stories. My parents were very much anti-church, but by showing your kindness to them, you changed their opinion on the Christian faith, and every week my brother would listen to your stories. Although I was avoiding you, I was still listening. Anyway, as you know my brother died and you completed the funeral service, and my parents were ever so grateful to you. But Mr. Wood, those Bible stories you told stayed with me, and you said that Jesus had come into the world to be our friend, and if we trust Him and believe in Him and ask Him to forgive us for our sins, He will grant us eternity with Him. For years I thought this was too simplistic, but it stayed with me for fifty years, and I want you to know that I have become a Christian because of you seeing my brother and telling him those Bible stories.'"

"Oh, Dad, that's wonderful!" I responded. "It coincides with messages from Isaiah that I am going to preach from." He asked me what passage it was and I said, "Isaiah 55 vs 10-11." I read it out to him.

*10 As the rain and the snow*
   *come down from heaven,*
*and do not return to it*
   *without watering the earth*
*and making it bud and flourish,*
      *so that it yields seed for the sower and bread for the*
*eater,*
*11 so is my word that goes out from my mouth:*
   *It will not return to me empty,*
*but will accomplish what I desire*
   *and achieve the purpose for which I sent it.*

For over 70 years Dad had been scattering the seed, in his school years, in his army years, in the ministry, in his family and even in the testimony he gave to the nurses in his dying days. Sometimes, he saw fruit and rejoiced, other times he saw none and persevered, and sometimes he saw it squashed and was discouraged. But this was a reminder to him that God is true to his word, that every time we open our mouths to speak about Christ, whether directly or indirectly, it will not be in vain. God will bring good out of it. All glory to Him!

A selection of James' sermons and additional photos can be found at
Awellspentjourney.co.uk

www.ingramcontent.com/pod-product-compliance
Ingram Content Group UK Ltd.
Pitfield, Milton Keynes, MK11 3LW, UK
UKHW052004201224
3801UKWH00017B/115